The Management of American Foundations:

Administration, Policies, and Social Role

Arnold J. Zurcher

New York University Press
New York   1972

To

Marie

361.76
2u8m
81482
Jan.1973

PREFACE

IN THE ENSUING DISCUSSION of the management of foundations,
I have considered the details of administrative structure and
behavior within the broader context of foundation policy and
operation. My aim has been to make the discussion informal
and nontechnical and to keep it focused as closely as possible
on the realities of the foundation scene. My approach is
selective, but I have not failed to give at least cursory treatment to every major aspect of foundation operation. If, moreover, some distortion of emphasis may have resulted because
of this selective and informal approach to the subject, there

may be compensation in the book's enhanced appeal to the nonprofessional reader.

Footnotes at the end of each chapter will indicate the range and nature of the sources upon which I have relied. I am especially indebted to the four editions of *The Foundation Directory*, to various government documents and reports, to the annual reports of certain foundations, to various issues of *Foundation News*, and to many of the authors who, over the years, have produced the rather impressive list of books on foundations published by Russell Sage Foundation. Chiefly, however, I have relied on observations derived from my experience of a quarter of a century as a foundation executive and trustee and on information and opinions offered by other foundation staff people and trustees with whom I associated during that period.

Much of Chapter 6, "Measuring the Success of a Foundation Grant," was first published in the March, 1970 issue of *Foundation News* under the title "Measuring the Product of a Foundation Grant," but the material of that chapter has since been somewhat revised. For some of the data on foundation personnel and trustees, I have used information accumulated and tabulated for the recently published study of the foundation administrator of which I was a co-author.

Many friends and professional colleagues were generous in extending assistance. In naming a number of them, and identifying the assistance they rendered, I wish to make it emphatically clear that none has any responsibility for the content and style of the volume or for the views expressed therein.

A former student of mine, and valued colleague in the study leading to the work on the foundation administrator, Jane Dustan, read the original version of the manuscript and, besides saving me from various errors, polished up the syntax. Miss Dustan is presently Associate for Program Development of the Association for the Aid of Crippled Children. Walter E. Ashley, another former student, formerly of the staff of the

Ford Foundation but more recently an executive of Mobil
Oil Corporation, read and criticized parts of the manuscript.
I have also exploited some of the data Dr. Ashley originally
assembled for his unpublished doctoral dissertation on the
world's largest private foundation. My son, Arnold J. Zurcher,
Jr., a member of the legal firm of Cadwalader, Wickersham
and Taft, generously assisted with certain sections of the book
dealing with public regulation. Harold S. Sloan, former Executive Director of the Alfred P. Sloan Foundation and now
President of the Institute for Instructional Improvement, a
scholar with whom I have had the honor of collaborating in
other ventures that led to considerable typesetting, provided
me with many helpful suggestions about the way in which
the content of the book might be presented and about the
content itself.

I was especially fortunate in persuading Donald R. Young
and F. Emerson Andrews to read the manuscript. Dr. Young,
a distinguished sociologist, is president emeritus and former
trustee of Russell Sage Foundation. Mr. Andrews is president
emeritus of The Foundation Center and one of the country's
leading authorities on foundations. Although neither offered
endorsement of any part of the manuscript, each of them
encouraged me to publish it and each of them saved me from
a number of serious factual errors.

Finally, I wish to pay tribute to the high editorial standards of the New York University Press. The application to
the manuscript of their editorial requirements improved the
readability of the volume.

                                                    A. J. Z.

CONTENTS

INTRODUCTION

ASTUTE OBSERVERS of the American foundation concur in the opinion that it has recently suffered a serious decline in public confidence. Some believe that perhaps foundations have reached the lowest point in public esteem since they became active at the beginning of the century. This loss of public confidence has been reflected in congressional and governmental policy. Since 1950 there have been three major congressional investigations. The first was led by Representative Eugene E. Cox of Georgia in 1952; the second, by Representative B. Carroll Reece of Tennessee in 1954; and the third and most recent, by Representative Wright Patman of Texas who, for the purpose, used a subcommittee of the House Select Committee on Small Business of which he was chairman. The Patman investigation was initiated in 1962 and continued throughout that decade, producing a number of "reports"— at least six—all of which were highly critical of foundations.[1] During the early sixties, moreover, the Treasury, undoubtedly influenced by the public furore created by Mr. Patman, brought out its own catalog of foundation shortcomings.[2] Although more restrained than Mr. Patman, the Treasury issued a report which constituted a severe indictment of some of the foundations. Indeed the severity was underscored by the report's very restraint and its suggestion for reform. Finally, in 1969, came the Tax Reform Act which those involved with foundations considered at least an implied indictment of foundations and convincing evidence of public distrust.

Most of the criticism thus recorded was inspired by overt abuses chargeable to those who resorted to foundations for private, nonphilanthropic purposes although the abuses usually were committed by individuals who controlled more or less little known foundations. Rarely were such abuses attributed to the leading foundations. But though these overt abuses were undoubtedly the immediate cause of the deterioration of the public's confidence in foundations, it is the contention of this volume that there is a more fundamental reason the public has lost confidence in foundations, for which the abuses are largely a symptom. This more fundamental reason is the fact that foundation directors have failed to achieve more efficient administration and more far-seeing management.

In the pages which follow, I will examine these failures in management, some cursorily, some at length. I will direct my attention especially towards such subjects as the government of foundations; staff weaknesses; deficiencies in the internal procedures which foundations follow to conduct their activities and make decisions; failures in communication with each other and the public; their handling of financial affairs;

and the quality of the foundation program. At appropriate intervals I will review the more overt abuses that have afflicted the foundation community, the recent efforts by government to curb such abuses, and the response of the administrators of the foundations to public criticism and government intervention. In a final chapter, I will consider the kind of philanthropy, uniquely appropriate to foundations, to which they might address themselves in the years immediately ahead if they wish to make a persuasive justification for survival.

Undoubtedly the reader will detect an underlying bias in favor of foundations, and to this I plead guilty. I believe that in an era which advances governmental and public hegemony in almost every area of human endeavor, it is desirable to maintain as large a degree of social pluralism in organization and policymaking as possible. It is particularly desirable to maintain an institution like the foundation because, among private institutions concerned with public ends, the foundation is peculiarly equipped to command the resources and the freedom of action to provide alternatives to governmental policy and, if it will, to take the lead in exploring new and uncharted directions in which society might move. All this, I believe, makes for a more open and a more enlightened society.

On the other hand, my prime objective has not been to praise the foundation in respect to either its past performance or its future promise. The prime objective has been to appraise it critically: to identify the shortcomings of management and personnel, survey steps that have been taken to remedy these, and to suggest other remedies. Along with other friends of the foundation, I am convinced that, unless foundations persuade the public that they are serious about overcoming their shortcomings and improving their performance, they are indeed in jeopardy. In any event, unless managerial reform is undertaken and prosecuted vigorously, it will be difficult for the foundation to remain a viable institution during the coming generation. It will certainly not be able to discharge the role of social and intellectual leadership that we have just suggested is especially appropriate to it.

NOTES FOR INTRODUCTION

1. For a critical assessment of the Patman investigations, see Andrews, *Patman and Foundations: Review and Assessment* (The Foundation Center, New York, 1968).
2. *Treasury Department Report on Private Foundations* (Washington, Government Printing Office, February, 1965).

THE PRIVATE FOUNDATION
—AN OVERVIEW

IN WRITING ABOUT foundations one of the principal obstacles encountered is the ambiguity that attends the use of the term. The term is often included in the names of fund-raising agencies, community welfare and patriotic societies, university and college alumni fund "development" units, church endowments, professional societies, trade associations, voluntary health organizations that conduct campaigns such as the "March of Dimes," and even of government departments and agencies which use tax revenues to support public and private educational, scientific, and cultural activities. As a result, the word "foundation" may identify many organizations that have only a very distant relationship with each other. This loose application of the term has caused much of the current confusion as to just what a foundation is and does. The confusion afflicts not only the press and public forums but congressional investigations and reports and sometimes even legislation and administrative regulations, including occasionally regulations of the Internal Revenue Service. To compound the confusion, organizations that have the right to use the term sometimes avoid using it in their formal name. Instead, they may be referred to with the word "fund," "corporation," "endowment," "trust," or even "association."

The type of foundation with which this book is concerned is a philanthropic organization that does not make appeals to the public for resources but has property and income of its own. Its property may be a portfolio of stocks, bonds, mortgages, and royalty agreements; or it may be real property or a business enterprise. In any case its wealth usually comes from a single source, such as a family or a corporation, and if it is derived from various sources, the property is likely to be the product of bequests or legacies which, for investment purposes, are administered as a single corpus. These resources, moreover, are sometimes used to finance certain public activities directly and the foundation might be classified as a special-purpose foundation. More often, its resources support many and varied organizations engaged in activities for the public good. This definition paraphrases a more succinct one provided by America's leading authority on the subject, Mr. F. Emerson Andrews. He defines the "foundation" treated in this volume as a "nongovernmental, nonprofit organization, having a principal fund of its own, managed by its own trustees or directors, and established to maintain or aid social, educational, charitable, religious or other activities serving the common welfare." [1]

In the Tax Reform Act of 1969, Congress sought for the first time to provide a definition of a foundation such as the one discussed here. The effort scarcely added lustre to the reputation of those who drew up the Act. This act describes in considerable detail those tax-exempt organizations that are *not* foundations and defines, at least by implication, the foundation substantially as Andrews does, namely, as a privately administered, tax-exempt charitable organization with an endowment or property providing at least two-thirds of its income.[2]

Andrews' concept of the foundation is an old one. Dr. Marion Fremont-Smith, one of the principal authorities on the legal aspects of the foundation, reminds us that perpetuities were established for religious purposes in early Egypt and in Chaldea; that associations of persons, called foundations, were encouraged during the first centuries of the Roman Empire and given the right to receive bequests in perpetuity to support worship and to aid the indigent; that similar foundations were established in the Mohammedan world; and that much American law affecting the foundation, including the corporate form of organization, the concept of charitable trusteeship, and the right to administer property in perpetuity, had its origin before the Conquest.[3] The foundation, as we are defining it, is clearly a venerable institution.

Nevertheless, foundations really did not proliferate until the twentieth century, in the United States. And this was due to the tradition of voluntarism, a generous government policy of tax exemption, and, above all, the maturation of the economy and creation of great fortunes. During the first seven decades of the century, the number of foundations, their wealth, and the scope of their largess have dwarfed any historical precedent and any activity by foundations created elsewhere. In those seven decades foundations in the United States have increased from approximately 50 * with assets of about 250 million dollars to some 26,000 in 1972 of which

* The first edition of *The Foundation Directory* (page xi) lists only ten foundations, founded before 1900, each of which had assets of at least one million dollars. When that edition was published, their total worth was 124 million dollars.

somewhat more than 5,450 met the requirements for inclusion in *The Foundation Directory*. They have assets worth at least 500,000 dollars and an annual volume of grants totalling at least 25,000 dollars.[4] These foundations held assets estimated at about 25 billion dollars and disbursed about 1.5 billion dollars annually.[5] Even if we allow for the serious monetary inflation which has continued throughout most of the period after 1940, the increase in the asset value of the foundations is impressive although as we shall note later, the total wealth of foundations is still a decidedly small fraction of the total national wealth.

At least one foundation large enough to claim a listing in *The Foundation Directory* exists in the District of Columbia and each of the states except Alaska, but 27 percent of the foundations in *The Directory* are located in New York State and for the most part these are in New York City. With some notable exceptions, they include the foundations with assets of greatest magnitude. Also all of the private agencies chiefly concerned with foundations, including The Foundation Center, the Council on Foundations, the National Council on Philanthropy, and Russell Sage Foundation are located in New York City.

Applicants for funds undoubtedly find the concentration of foundations in New York City a convenience. The concentration also makes it convenient for foundation staff members to communicate with each other—if they have a mind to do so. But the concentration also has drawbacks. Critics hint darkly of a "foundation establishment" and decry the preponderant influence of the foundation executives over the nation's cultural, scientific, and educational values. Foundations that are located in New York are required to respond to a disproportionate share of the criticism directed against all foundations by politicians and the public. The leaders of the New York foundations would probably be the first to agree that all foundations would benefit from a broader and more balanced geographical distribution of wealth and influence.

Since geographical concentration facilitates communication among foundations, it should also stimulate cooperative effort, but foundations traditionally have preferred "to go it alone." In part this is due to the fact that their founders have sought to prevent any dilution of their oft-circumscribed, and sometimes eccentric, policy objectives, but it also reflects a fear, dating back to the "trust busting" era and the early investigations. The first was conducted by a committee headed by Frank P. Walsh, which had been created by Congress in August 1912. The report of that committee suggested that, if foundations acted in concert even in minor matters, they might be accused of being a "money trust" and of using their economic power in ways that would be detrimental to the public interest. In more recent years such accusations have also been made by the Patman Committee and by periodicals of the New Left [6] and, though exaggerated, they have not lacked some basis in fact.

Despite this tradition of individualism, a few of the more mature general-purpose foundations have made some attempts to cooperate with each other during the past two decades. Professional staffs of these foundations maintain informal communication. As we shall see later, they have created *ad hoc* organizations for the exchange of ideas. They comment informally on each other's programs and projects, exchange appraisals of projects and make efforts to avoid duplicating each other's projects. Increasingly two or more foundations have come to share responsibility for a project, the purposes being to distribute the financial burden, lend the project the prestige of cooperative foundation sponsorship, and make the greater expertise of more than one staff available.

Congressional investigators, such as Representatives Cox and Reece, have also stimulated the foundations to act together in setting up agencies to inform the public at large, and the information media, about foundations and what they do and do not do. Up to this point, The Foundation Center is probably the most elaborate and certainly the most successful organization that has been created for this purpose. It was established in the early 1950s at the initiative of the Carnegie Corporation, which made the first grant. Subsequently that grant was supplemented by grants from other large foundations. The Center's formally appointed task was to combat the secrecy that prevails among foundations, and its first President, F. Emerson Andrews, logically defined a corollary duty as that of encouraging foundations to publish reports about themselves. In view of these developments it is possible that the period of "splendid isolation" for foundations is nearing an end.

Legally a foundation is usually either a trust or a corporation. A foundation having the form of a trust is the product of an indenture, will, or similar instrument drawn up for philanthropic purposes by an individual (or institution) who donates the assets, identifies the purpose of the trust, and names the original trustees. Historically the trust was the more usual legal form of foundation and The Foundation Center estimates that probably a third of all current foundations still are trusts. Today, however, the corporate form of the foundation has become more popular. The corporation is established by a charter, granted by public authority, that identifies the legal existence of the foundation and specifies its powers and purposes. Congress has provided the corporate charters for a few foundations such as the General Education Board and the Carnegie Foundation for the Advancement of Teaching, but the overwhelming majority of corporate foundations are the product of a state authority, once the legislature, but nowadays an appropriate state administrative department.

Whatever significance the distinction between a trust and a corporation may have had historically, that distinction has become increasingly academic. As Mrs. Fremont-Smith suggests, courts are less concerned than they were formerly by the form of organization of a foundation when they rule on acceptable standards of fiduciary responsibility and behavior. They are relying increasingly on the stronger rules of equitable trust law and less on standards derived from the law of profit-making corporations.[7] Indeed, about half of the states apply the law of charitable trusts to charitable corporations, and foundations organized as charitable corporations are regarded as essentially instruments to administer charitable trusts. Hence to identify the directors of a charitable corporation as "trustees" does not betoken semantic confusion but an effort to describe the directors' legal responsibility. Dr. Fremont-Smith has suggested that corporate foundation directors be called "quasi-trustees" because they do possess the attributes of "regular trustees" but, unlike the stewards of a trust, they are not subjected to some of the more "stringent supervisory powers of the probate courts. . . ."[8]

The single individual, or family, is the usual source of foundation endowment, and they have established a wide variety of foundations, from an organization with limited assets and virtually no program, except making gifts to local charities, to an organization of great wealth, with a diversified program of giving. There are also a few family foundations that belong to the category we have previously labelled "special-purpose." The fund set up by Benjamin Franklin in 1790 to provide loans to artisans and apprentices of "good character" could be classified as special purpose, as can foundations created to defend and propagate the ideas of some economist or religious teacher, for example, or those created to maintain a bird sanctuary or a sanitarium for tubercular patients or to support the development of the hotel industry.

The other two principal sources of foundation resources are either a particular business or industrial enterprise or many small donations, legacies, or trusts intended to benefit the people of a particular community. A foundation financed by a business or industrial concern is called a business-based or business-sponsored foundation. A foundation used to disburse the incomes of many small trusts or legacies for projects within a limited geographical area is known as a community foundation.

However we may classify foundations, all benefit from

tax exemption. Also those who contribute to a foundation enjoy tax-deduction privileges; that is, they can use their contributions to reduce their own tax liability. These privileges have been extended by government because a foundation is considered to be a charitable, nonprofit, enterprise the contributions of which to charity reduce the expenditure which government itself would otherwise have to make. Exemption from state and local impositions may be important to a foundation; but it is the exemption from tax demands of the federal government that is of major significance, for these taxes are far more burdensome. It is for this reason that foundations have a far greater concern about the tax policy of the federal government and generally give more attention to the tax and financial regulations of the Internal Revenue Service than they do to the financial or other regulations issued by the states which created them.

Foundations first were exempted from paying income taxes in the abortive federal income-tax law of 1894. The exemption also was written into the first income-tax law to meet the test of constitutionality, passed in 1913. In the decade that followed, Congress not only assured foundations freedom from the payment of other taxes but also evolved the policy of allowing donors to make tax free contributions to a foundation under estate and gift-tax laws and to include contributions to a foundation in the allowable charitable deductions from the income tax.[9] At the outset, moreover, and for a good many years, the government treated foundations—which, for the most part, are "holders" and "disbursers" of charitable funds and not "users"—exactly as they did the "users" of such funds, the schools, universities, hospitals, and similar institutions, which, in Treasury jargon are "501 (c) (3) organizations" that is, organizations identified in Section 501 (c) (3) of the Internal Revenue Code of 1954 as

"Corporations and any community chest, fund, or foundation, organized and operated exclusively for religious, charitable, scientific, testing for public safety, literary, or educational purposes, or for the prevention of cruelty to children or animals, no part of the net earnings of which inures to the benefit of any private shareholder or individual, no substantial part of the activities of which is carrying on propaganda, or otherwise attempting, to influence legislation, and which does not participate in, or intervene in (including the publishing or distributing statements), any political campaign on behalf of any candidate for public office."

Congress began to single out foundations for special and less-favorable treatment in 1964 when it allowed prospective donors to deduct as much as 30 percent from their adjusted gross income for contributions to certain "users" of philanthropy, such as universities and hospitals, but maintained the 20 percent maximum permissible deduction for foundations. In 1969, the first tax was levied on foundations at the rate of 4 percent of income. This, of course, is by far the most significant indication that foundations might experience less-favorable tax treatment than heretofore and less-favorable treatment than any other charitable enterprise. Legislators apparently considered the tax a routine imposition and could therefore regard it as a precedent to justify the levying of further taxes.

Because of the relatively generous tax treatment which, up to now, the government has accorded foundations, federal tax policy may be said to have stimulated the growth of foundations both in number and in assets. A sense of social trusteeship of great wealth may have been the principal, if not the exclusive, motive of men such as Carnegie or Rockefeller [10] when they established their foundations and it is practically certain that such a motive also influenced most of the more recent creators of foundations—men like Alfred P. Sloan, Jr., or members of the Ford family. At the same time, it is also fairly certain that these latter two and others who have contributed to the number of foundations established since the 1930s and especially since World War II were not uninfluenced by the government's tax policy, that permitted them to escape death or inheritance duties, enjoy other tax exemptions, and acquire tax advantages.

A second consequence of the evolving fiscal relationship of the federal government and foundations is a growing regulatory power over foundations. As was pointed out earlier, with very few exceptions, foundations are created or chartered under state law in the United States, and the states may regulate them. However, because of its taxing powers, the federal government has become the foundations' principal or, at least, most effective regulatory agency. From 1934, when the formal prohibition of the use of foundation resources to influence legislation and carry on propaganda was established, until the present time, the volume of federal regulation of foundation activities has grown apace and, as will be discussed in Chapter 11, has been heavily supplemented in the Tax Reform Act.

Such, in brief, are some of the more important general considerations to be kept in mind concerning the private foundation. Hopefully, the reader will gain a clearer picture of the foundation than that afforded by this formal and somewhat legalistic description, as we proceed now to review and appraise, in some detail, the foundation's conduct and management and its cultural and intellectual role.

NOTES—CHAPTER 1

1. Introduction to *The Foundation Directory*, 2nd Edition (New York, 1964), p. 9.
2. Tax Reform Act, Section 101 (a); Code, Section 509.
3. *Foundations and Government* (New York, 1965), pp. 14 *ff. passim.*

4. Statistics from Introduction to *The Foundation Directory*, 4th Edition, p. vii.
5. 4th Edition, p. x.
6. See, for example, letter of transmittal, *Patman Committee Report*, First Installment, December 31, 1962, p.v, and the issue of *Ramparts Magazine* (July, 1969).
7. See her "Duties and Powers of Charitable Fiduciaries: The Law of Trusts and the Correction of Abuses," *UCLA Law Review*, Vol. XII, No. 4 (May, 1966), p. 1044. But see also her comparison of foundation corporations and trusts in her *Foundations and Government* (New York, 1965), pp. 154-157, in which she indicates that some distinction between corporate and trust foundations persist and have practical importance.
8. *Foundations and Government*, p. 130.
9. The more important steps in the evolution of early federal tax policy towards foundations are traced in Fremont-Smith, *Foundations and Government*, p. 65.
10. See Andrew Carnegie, *The Gospel of Wealth and Other Timely Essays* (New York, 1900), and Nevins, *John D. Rockefeller, the Heroic Age of American Business* (New York, 1940).

Chapter 2

THE FAMILY FOUNDATION

IN *The Foundation Directory*, foundations bearing individual or family names outnumber those bearing community or other institutional names by a ratio of almost nine to one. In some cases even a foundation that bears an institutional name is the product of an individual or family endowment, an excellent illustration being the well-known Twentieth Century Fund established by Edward A. Filene, the Boston merchant. With a few exceptions, on which we shall comment later, the endowment of a family foundation is quite modest and usually remains so. Only a few more than one-fifth of the 26,000 foundations, estimated to have been in existence in 1972, the vast majority of which were family foundations, either had an initial endowment of at least 500,000 dollars or grew to have such an endowment. These foundations account for more than 90 percent of all foundation wealth. The remaining four-fifths of existing foundations have very limited wealth—startlingly limited in view of the popular assumption that all foundations are wealthy and even "super-rich." A few years ago, F. Emerson Andrews sampled some 10,500 foundations that were too small to be included in *The Foundation Directory*, and he found that the average asset value of each was 37,000 dollars, accounting for total assets of only 388 million dollars.[1]

The administration of a new family foundation is anything but complicated. Usually the founder installs himself or some relative or retainer as board chairman or "chief executive officer" of the foundation. He then nominates family members, the family lawyer, personal friends and business and professional associates to the necessary board of trustees and engages whatever operating personnel may be needed—usually none. Often the foundation has no quarters of its own. Its official address may be the family lawyer's office, or a bank or just a post office box.

There are several reasons why so many family foundations come into being and persist indefinitely. As a conduit for the donor's or the family's charities they offer certain advantages. At the end of a taxable year, for example, funds that can be expended for charity do not have to be handed over immediately to the ultimate users but can be transferred to the foundation and distributed more gradually, an opportunity thus being provided for weighing the relative merits of possible recipients. A second, more subjective but none the less important reason, is the desire to perpetuate the philanthropic reputation of the donor or the family. Still another reason for creating a family foundation has been the hope of securing certain economic advantages, some of them distinctly

nonphilanthropic in character, most of which have been fore-
closed by the Tax Reform Act of 1969. Indeed, because of its
passage and its restriction of tax and other advantages to foundation founders, it is possible that the small family foundation
will cease to be as attractive as it once was and that fewer
family foundations will be created or maintained.

Because most foundations have a family origin, it is not
surprising that almost all of the larger foundations, that is,
the 331 which in 1972 had assets of 10 million dollars or
more, and the 1,841 which in the same year had assets between 1 and 10 million dollars [2] are family foundations. Relatively few community- and company-sponsored foundations
command resources of this magnitude. A few of the family-
originated foundations that have this level of wealth were
well endowed at the beginning of their existence. The Carnegie
Corporation, the early Rockefeller creations, and Russell Sage
Foundation were initially rather generously endowed and were
relatively large to begin with. Most of the larger family-
originated foundations, however, started with modest assets
and grew larger.

A foundation with only a modest endowment to begin
with may be transformed into one with considerable resources
within a comparatively short time as the result of the death
of a founding family member and the transfer of a large
estate or it may take place more gradually. An example of the
first is the Ford Foundation. It began its corporate life in
1936, without assets of significance, and was used to support
the local charities of the Ford family. Then, at the end of the
1940s, when Edsel Ford, and later his father, Henry, died,
the foundation was given a multi-billion dollar endowment
and became the largest of all private foundations. An equally
startling and more recent example of sudden transformation
from modest wealth to great affluence was offered at the
end of 1971 when it was announced that the Robert Wood
Johnson Foundation, of New Brunswick, New Jersey which,
until that time, had been engaged in supporting local health

institutions, had been given assets of more than a billion dollars by the will of its founder, a gift which raised it to second rank among all foundations.[3]

An example of the second, or more gradual rise to considerable wealth, is afforded by the Alfred P. Sloan Foundation. The founder originally donated 500,000 dollars when the foundation was created in 1934, and, some years later, 10 million more. For some time thereafter, Mr. Sloan, his wife, and certain of their personal holding companies regularly made tax deductible gifts out of income which were added to the corpus. In 1947, the Sloan Foundation received its only "outside" donation—an unusual event in the life of a family foundation—when it was given approximately 1.5 million dollars by General Motors dealers throughout the United States in honor of Mr. Sloan. By 1955, the assets of the foundation totalled a quite respectable 78 million dollars. A year later, following the transfer of funds from the estate of Mrs. Sloan, they totalled almost 146 million dollars. At the time of Mr. Sloan's death in 1966, a sizable portion of his estate was distributed directly to certain institutions in which he had a personal interest, but a relatively modest portion also was transferred to the foundation to bring its assets at the time close to 300 million dollars, and the value of this foundation's endowment has remained around that amount.

In view of the opportunity, under existing gift and estate tax laws, to make tax-free transfers of property to a foundation, and the further opportunity, under existing income tax laws, to direct allowable charitable deductions—or at least a large share of them—to one's foundation, foundations probably will be established in the way the Ford, Johnson, or Sloan foundations have been. They probably will be started with small endowments and then expanded. It is less likely that foundations will be set up with generous endowments from the start, as were some of those created earlier in the century.

The Intermediate Family Foundation

As the donor makes additional gifts to his foundation, and the recipients of grants become less local, a foundation may be said to have reached an "intermediate" stage between the primitive family organization and what will be described later as a mature, general-purpose foundation. At this stage, the board of trustees may be broadened somewhat although the membership is not likely to include others than the donor's circle of business associates and personal friends or his family. Occasionally one or two full-time staff people may be employed who become active in all phases of the foundation's activity, both in its internal administration and in the making of grants. It is equally possible that the foundation, at this stage, will continue to operate without paid hands and remain a donor-controlled foundation. This may be the case even though, in some instances, the foundation's wealth may reach a level above 100 million dollars or even several times that amount. Thus much of the administrative structure of the foundation when it was first established often persists at this intermediate stage. Especially persistent may be the influence of the founder-donor. Policies are likely to be dictated by him and the recipients of grants selected by him. The effect of this dominance upon trustee associates and staff, if there is any staff, is hardly salutary. The trustees tend to ignore their legal responsibility to exercise their individual judgment and become "yes men." They calm their conscience with the slogan that "it is his money" and go along with whatever the founder or his representative wants to do, so long as it does not violate the law. Any existing staff members are prone to become sycophants, quite ready to justify the ideas and desires of the foundation's leadership and quite unlikely, themselves, to exercise any real administrative or philanthropic discretion.

The influence of a strong-willed founder-donor may even survive his death and exert a kind of psychological mortmain upon trustees and staff associated with him during his lifetime. These seek to perpetuate his ideas and even his idiosyncrasies and to continue his philanthropic policies. Rubber stamps during the founder-donor's lifetime, they continue as rubber stamps for a ghost. Certainly this is not generally true, and it may not be true even in a sizable minority of cases; but it is true enough in far too many instances.

Founder-donor and family influence at the primitive foundation level is normally tolerated by society without too much criticism—at least as respects the foundation's bona fide charitable activities. However, when the foundation reaches an intermediate stage and commands the resources to influence social causes, at least somewhat, some people begin to look askance at donor control and to question whether the relationship between the donor and his foundation should not be cut.

The franker of such critics list a number of rather persuasive objections. For one thing they find it difficult, if not logically impossible, to reconcile the continuing influence and control over a charity held by a donor to a foundation that has achieved a major economic status with the fact that members of the general public must surrender all control over the modest gifts they make to charity—to the Red Cross, for example, or to the community United Fund. The foundation donor's special prerogative of disposing of his wealth a second time seems especially objectionable when, as is now generally the case, he has been forgiven taxes he would have been compelled to pay if he had not exercised the privilege of dedicating the funds, at first, to a private foundation.

Another objection of the critics is the fact that the donor is sometimes an eccentric who insists that the foundation devote its resources to the promotion of causes that are hardly in the public interest. The political and social views which he espouses and recommends are usually derived from an earlier generation and may be quite "Gothic" in nature. Sometimes the views thus disseminated are of an extremist nature, often either of the far right or the far left. In any case, if the donor refuses to accept the concept that the proper educational role of a foundation in a liberal, democratic society is to stimulate debate on issues and not to inculcate a narrow sectarianism, the critics complain that the donor or the associates whom he influences and directs closely approach, and sometimes overstep, the limits of what constitutes overt propaganda and legislative lobbying.

Still a third, and probably the most important, objection is the delay in developing two principal attributes of any private institution devoted to public purposes, namely, a board of trustees that can exercise the kind of independent judgment the law demands and a staff that can introduce professional judgment on grants and appropriate administrative procedures. As we have already noted, continued founder-donor control makes such a development difficult if not impossible.

But there are other observers who insist that there are advantages to donor or family control of a foundation at the intermediate level and that these may offset the liabilities. For example, the participation of the founder-donor, or someone close to him, in the foundation's counsels can have a salutary administrative influence. Such participation may discourage overstaffing, unnecessary internal administrative expenses, and unnecessary conferences, "field trips," and similar activities of which the more professional foundations that are not controlled by a donor are sometimes guilty. Administrative frugality, thus enforced, is to be commended—so it is urged—even though the founder-donor occasionally may carry it to such an extent that the most conventional type of philanthropic program suffers as a result.

Then, too, there are those who maintain that the philanthropic program which a donor of an intermediate foundation is likely to support needs to be encouraged if the full spectrum of philanthropic needs is to be met. The intermediate foundation under donor control usually engages in conventional supportive philanthropy. It tenders its support to exist-ing institutions. It looks with favor on grants for equipment for schools, colleges, universities, and medical centers, and even contributes to their operational budgets. It supports scholars, writers, researchers, and artists, sometimes for considerable periods. The founder-donor may also concentrate the gifts of the foundation upon a few institutions that he thinks are well and honorably managed. He will rationalize such a policy by condemning what he calls "scatteration," that is, diffusion of largess among many recipients in relatively small amounts and for relatively brief periods. Those who do this are probably not a majority but they are a significant number.

It can be argued that supportive philanthropy of this kind does not require a foundation instrument. The aid might be provided as well, and sometimes with greater dispatch, by direct donation or by testamentary gift. This is undoubtedly true. At the same time it can also be argued that as long as a would-be benefactor sees an advantage in setting up a founda-tion to dispense his largess, and the government encourages him to do so or at least does not discourage him, the inter-mediate family foundation under donor control will have to be tolerated if not encouraged. Otherwise private support of the nation's educational and cultural institutions could decline significantly either because the wealthy foundations emerging from donor control are less sympathetic towards such phil-anthropy or because more of the money that might otherwise have gone into the intermediate type of foundation is siphoned off in taxes.

Those who hold a brief for donor control of an inter-mediate foundation also remind us that whatever the reputa-tion some donors may have, there have been others who were major philanthropic innovators. In what might be called the heroic period of American foundations, roughly from the beginning of the twentieth century to the middle of the 1930s, those who endowed foundations are said to have been among the more creative of philanthropic policymakers. Men like Andrew Carnegie, the first and second Rockefellers, and Julius Rosenwald did indeed use their foundations for decidedly constructive purposes. They established famous universities, such as Chicago and Rockefeller, and schools of public health at Johns Hopkins and Harvard; they were instrumental in making revolutionary changes in medical education and research; they created a model retirement pension plan for college professors; they sought to improve community cultural standards by setting up libraries; they sought diligently for the day when the Negro and other minorities might enjoy rights on a par with the white man; and they supported research into endemic disease in various parts of the world. Supporters of donor control also identify more recent examples of innovative and imaginative philanthropy such as Alfred P. Sloan's creation of the cancer research center at the Memorial Hospital in New York or the Guggenheim's support of aviation and the rocket pioneer, Dr. Robert H. Goddard. Though advised by men like Embree, Rose, Gates, Flexner, and others of major stature, it is probably true that much of the initiative in this constructive pioneering of the private foundation is to be attributed to these founder-donors. They exercised this initiative through their foundations while these were still in an intermediate stage of development and largely under their personal control.

Any discussion of donor influence and close family control of an intermediate foundation thus has its pros and cons. In setting off the debits against the credits, some will conclude that public policy should not coddle an intermediate foundation under the control of donor or founding family. Others will bemoan the passing of family "proprietorship" of foundations as vigorously as they lament the passing of "owner management" of large business enterprises.

The Family General-Purpose Foundation

Those who may be unhappy with the conditions governing an intermediate type of foundation may derive some
satisfaction from the knowledge that time frequently trans-
forms it into a more mature, professionally oriented foundation. Family control is greatly reduced or practically overcome, except—in some instances—for the influence maintained
through the foundation's endowment, which, of course, is
difficult to neutralize. A point may be reached when the family
representative announces his immediate "abdication" from the
role of family steward and declines, thenceforth, to exercise
even nominal influence over the decisions of staff and trustees.
Normally the transformation is gradual and almost imper-
ceptible. At first, perhaps, a career staff man may be employed,
or maybe individuals who seek employment as philanthropic
experts in program matters or internal administration exclusively; that is, they are not employed because they "knew"
the donor or had influence with the donor's family or friends.
An effort is made to employ experts who can identify socially
rewarding areas for philanthropic investment. A policy is
adopted to stop making supportive institutional grants in favor
of grants for limited term, and categorically defined, projects
and to divert funds away from miscellaneous causes or from
the support of specific institutions and direct them towards
activities in rather carefully delimited fields. These, and other
comparable developments, indicate that an intermediate family
foundation has reached the status of a more seasoned, general-
purpose, professionally-managed one. A family representative
may still sit on the board or even serve as board chairman,
although, in theory, and usually in fact, his influence over the
foundation is no greater than that of any one of his colleagues.
There are probably not more than forty such foundations,
and most of them have considerable wealth; a very few have

great wealth. It is these general-purpose foundations and foundations of the intermediate type that will be the principal concern of subsequent chapters.

NOTES—CHAPTER 2

1. *The Foundation Directory*, 3rd Edition, p. 16.
2. *Ibid.*, 4th Edition, p. xv.
3. *New York Times* (Dec. 6, 1971).

Chapter 3

THE FOUNDATION'S TRUSTEES

ROBERT MULREANY, who has served on and written about foundation boards, delineates the responsibility of foundation trustees in some detail. A trustee or director and his associates are responsible for spending the foundation's income imaginatively, for investing and reinvesting its funds as a prudent man would invest his own property, and for managing the foundation's affairs in a "business-like manner." Mr. Mulreany also indicates that board members have an immediate and almost personal responsibility for making grants, their duties requiring them to "carefully investigate all requests for grants and all programs proposed for support"; to review grants already made and funded projects to see if the attendant conditions are being fulfilled; and to keep the public informed periodically on the foundation's activities.[1]

Technically this is a correct description of a trustee's duties for the board of which he is a member is indeed responsible for all facets of policy and operation. On the other hand, if taken literally, Mr. Mulreany's outline of duties could involve a trustee rather intimately in the details of administration rather than reserving for him the supervisory and policy-determining role normally associated with a board. In practice, of course, the foundation trustee's role varies widely. Depending upon the type of foundation—whether a primitive family, intermediate, general-purpose, or other foundation—he may exercise little influence over policy and confine himself to the details of administration; or he may combine administrative and policy roles; or again, he may serve on a board that confines itself to basic managerial decisions and keep relatively aloof from administrative matters.

As suggested earlier, while the founder of a foundation remains alive, we have the typical form of "family governance." The founder usually continues to direct the enterprise and makes the real decisions and his direction may continue even when the foundation reaches an intermediate stage of development. We have identified such a foundation as "donor-controlled" or "donor-administered." Under such a regimen, a trustee's role is likely to be that of "advising and assenting." He is denied, or denies himself, the true managerial or policy-making role that should be his.

As we have also noted earlier, even after the founder disappears from the scene, a trustee may not undertake the responsibilities for the management of the foundation that the law formally expects of him and his colleagues. He may insist he has a moral responsibility to adhere to the donor's policy or supposed policy. In another situation his discretion may have been circumscribed if the donor, in creating the foundation, set up a trust that is quite specific as to the allocation of resources and possibly even as to what investments the foundation may make. In either case the trustee has little, if any, opportunity to make decisions of any substantive significance. Moreover, in these circumstances, the foundation is slow to acquire staff and a trustee himself may continue to perform the duties that others might delegate to staff employees. Although he discharges, at least nominally, the supervisory and directorial role which the law assumes is his, his real role is an operational one. He participates in the administration of the foundation, and the foundation itself is appropriately described as a "trustee-administered" entity.

The usual conception of a trustee as one who supervises and makes basic decisions is more closely approximated in the cases of the older and more sizable intermediate and professional general-purpose foundations. These foundations may employ some staff, and operational duties can be delegated. The trustee can, if he will, restrict himself to exercising, with his colleagues, broad powers of supervision and deciding all major issues of policy. It is these foundations, therefore, that provide the true testing ground for an effective trustee. In them he encounters an intellectual challenge of a complexity that confronts few, if any, boards of other eleemosynary institutions. In matters of philanthropic policy he may be asked to decide on programs and major projects of a highly technical and novel character. He must determine whether they will advance knowledge or the arts or improve social conditions. From time to time he may be called upon to consider updating the foundation's philanthropy and redirecting resources into new and relatively unexplored channels. Such decisions require sophisticated judgment based on at least some personal investigation or direct knowledge and, above all, on the ability to assimilate and understand the brief of staff and other experts.

The sad fact is that far too many board members are unwilling or unable to discharge such a responsibility. Some of these may become complaisant and ratify what they do not understand allowing the staff expert to carry the real if not the formal responsibility for the decision. Others may become obstreperous, responding with a "gut" negative reaction, one vindicated by the opinions of a current golfing companion or of a fellow director on some corporate industrial board.

Still others, especially those serving on a board dominated by business and financial men, will forgo serious thought on program matters and concern themselves solely with managing the foundation's investment portfolio. Most members of any board, even those not recruited from the world of industry and banking, are convinced that they have the necessary expertise. And, fortunately for them, should their opinion of themselves not be absolutely correct, they can work closely with special investment counsel drawn from trust departments of banks, from the management of industrial pension funds, from those who manage the investments of universities and insurance companies, and from the bank that serves as investment counsel for the foundation. Unfortunately, perhaps, trustees tend to sequester themselves on an investment or finance committee and become virtually autonomous in their operation. The remaining members of the board have no more to do with investment policy or financial issues than they have with philanthropic issues or policy: They ratify the *fait accompli* of the committee—if indeed they are called upon to do even that.

Since final authority resides in the trustees, the quality of a foundations program will be determined, in considerable measure, by the degree of dedication and the intellectual level of the board. Especially is this true of the advanced, professionally-staffed, foundations. To secure trustees of high calibre, to enlist their interest, and to make their roles more meaningful and hence more useful, are among the major challenges that currently confront such foundations. These would find it profitable to expend much more thought and energy than they have in trying to satisfy such challenges. A more effective board could help considerably in improving internal administration. It could maintain a desirable equilibrium between the enthusiasm of the staff expert and the more conventional desires of the public. It could inject the more pragmatic considerations into discussions about the foundation's existing and future philanthropic policy and it could disabuse the public about such often firmly held beliefs that foundations are not concerned with the general welfare or that they are instruments to take advantage of the tax laws.

During the years the Alfred P. Sloan Foundation was maturing, its founder engaged in one or two experiments to create a more effective and useful board. By and large his ideas were derived from his business experience with the General Motors Corporation. One was to have staff members sit as board members along with "outsiders" so that staff men would be considered as equals by board members from outside the foundation. Hopefully this would foster a more truly bilateral exchange between staff and board, and thus, to an extent at least, aid in overcoming the hindrances to communication and the rather arbitrary separation of amateur and expert which organizational dichotomy reinforces. The experiment was not successful and it was eventually liquidated because it enhanced the dominant position of the staff expert. It did not result in greater board involvement in determining foundation policy or improve the quality of board discussion and decisions. Mr. Sloan also created special trustee committees to review proposed grants in certain areas the foundation was supporting. These committees were always headed by a staff person who was also a board member. Again the idea did not work. Inevitably the staff man dominated the sittings of the mixed committee—at least when talking "shop"—simply because he had his clipboard and his memoranda and the board members did not. In time this idea was also abandoned.

A somewhat similar effort to make board service more meaningful was undertaken by the Julius Rosenwald Fund. In this instance the effort apparently met with some success.

At any rate, those who tell the story of that historic foundation state that its board's executive committee and many other trustees "were in such immediate touch with the various projects that, regardless of legal division of function, trustees and officers worked in close cooperation both in formulating policy and in operations." [2] The difficulty with the Rosenwald experiment, however, as with the Sloan experience is that they can hardly be applied to any but the intermediate family foundations still under the influence of a strong founder. Moreover, the Rosenwald Fund was essentially an "operational" foundation that supported programs of long duration —long enough for even the laymen on the board to become familiar with them. Normally, the trustees of the general-purpose foundation cannot do this.

For that and other foundations, part of the answer to the demand for a more competent and useful board would be to appoint younger people. Far too many foundations continue trustees well past normal retirement age. Many have boards with a minority of members—and sometimes a majority—in their late seventies and even in their eighties. Although it does not necessarily follow that the members are physically or mentally incompetent, or that the board will become senile, it too often insures that the board will be inflexible in its thinking, inhospitable to new ideas, unsympathetic to new intellectual and cultural trends, and generally removed from the mainstream of social development—all qualities guaranteed to put it at a disadvantage with the staff or the public.

Retirement requirements quickly solve the problem of removing old trustees although some trusts stipulate that trustees may serve during their lifetime, and even where discretion exists, boards dislike to send senior members packing. One foundation of size sought to overcome this sentimental obstacle by stipulating that, although most trustees must retire at 72, they could continue as members of a "trustee advisory committee," attend and speak at meetings, but could not vote. If a five-minute guillotine closure rule could also be placed

in effect for members of such a committee, when an arrange-
ment of this kind is set up, this might be an acceptable com-
promise solution between keeping older men around and
bringing younger men on the board and transferring power
to them. As matters stand, too few foundations of magnitude
have a formal retirement policy or maintain any customary
role that rids them of trustees before they reach an age that
threatens senility.

Another contribution to a more effective board would
be to recruit trustees representing the various professions, and
various social strata, thereby broadening a board's expertise
and social outlook. Unfortunately it is generally true that even
when professional persons are appointed, the action is seldom
an expression of policy. Rather it is the result of some direct
personal association with an influential board member, or
perhaps with the founder or the founder's family. The
physician on the board is often the founder's personal physician; the lawyer, a member of the firm which handled the
founder's estate; and the university president, the head of the
founder's alma mater or of the alma mater of some senior
board member. Moreover, the lawyer, academician, or doctor
who is appointed, usually is an administrator in his particular
profession or discipline. He is not a teacher, researcher, or
practitioner. Nor has there been any serious effort among
foundations to recruit "anti-establishment" personnel, that is,
representatives of the more unorthodox areas of society to
serve on boards. As one critic has reminded us recently, foundation boards normally contain no Negroes, women, social
workers, ministers, active scientists, scholars, or engineers.[3]

A principal reason why foundation boards are relatively
unrepresentative is the almost universal practice of coopting
new members. An existing board tends to fill vacancies with
individuals who share the interests and experiences of incumbents and with whom the incumbents feel "comfortable." For
some observers. Dr. Donald Young for example, the resulting
compatibility of membership is considered desirable, espe-

cially in the case of the smaller foundations.[4] On the other hand it is also true that too great a degree of compatibility, and too similar a social outlook, can be a liability. It is differences in sex, age, race, social status, and professional background among board members that offer the best guarantee that boards will broaden their social outlook and that differences and conflicting points of view will be considered seriously and reconciled, if possible.

Those who have explored the possibility of qualifying the system of cooption and overcoming, at least to a degree, its undesirable influence on the composition of boards and on the behavior of board members, usually recommend that the general public be represented. Choosing public members might follow the precedent established in some states of having the governor, or some other official, serve *ex officio* on university and other eleemosynary boards; or it might take the form of an appointment by the attorney general of the state or by some comparable official.

Whatever means were taken to place representatives of the public on boards, statutory and charter changes would be required and the incidental delay and procedural complexities would raise a question as to their practicability. But even if the effort to place public members on boards were successful, the results would probably be disappointing. The personal qualifications, including the intellectual qualifications, of appointees would probably be even less satisfactory than the qualifications of persons selected by cooption by the board membership. Additionally, bringing the state and its officials so directly into the inner organizational structure of a foundation might well mark the beginning of the decay of the foundation as a privately managed, autonomous, philanthropic agency. These objections might be overcome, however, if a list of nominees for board membership were compiled by members of the bench or by some other officials; the foundation board could then make the actual choices from this list. This would avoid the dangers of outright governmental designation of members of foundation boards. It might also be possible to introduce such a plan informally without resort to complicated and long drawn out statutory or charter changes.

Other, less debatable and less fundamental, changes in organization or procedure might be exploited to involve board members more intimately in policy-making activity and thus help to make an indifferent board more effective. Several major foundations have found that it was advantageous to reduce the number of board meetings held each year, but to extend the length of each session to two or three days to introduce more trustees into the intricacies of thinking and planning. It is likely that, over a period of several days, even the most unpromising trustee would find it incumbent to do a little homework, avoid "gut" reactions to ideas, and attempt, instead, to appreciate the intricacies of a problem and inform himself of the alternatives available to him in disposing of the problem. On such occasions it would be possible, too, for staff members to indulge in something intellectually more satisfying than merely advocating some project. The staff man could review the broader areas of foundation activity, indulge in some forecasting as to what the philanthropic priorities are likely to be in the decade ahead, and possibly even engage in a fruitful dialogue with board members.

Giving the staff greater discretion in committing the foundation to specific grants could also free boards of much of the minutiae that normally clutter up agenda and give them more time for consideration of the larger issues of policy. This can be done—and in some cases has been done—by establishing in advance a clear understanding of the kinds of broad programs to which money may be allocated and authorizing appropriations which set limits on what may be spent on particular programs. Such staff discretion must, of course, be supplemented by machinery to monitor and appraise programs and projects from time to time, the results of which would be available to the board or to a board committee. If these steps were taken, a board could reserve to itself the power to authorize only the very largest grants, delegating authority for other grants and limited appropriations to a staff committee headed by the foundation's president or executive director.

Associated with the problem of attracting competent men to serve on a board is the question of payment. Emerson Andrews [5] found that foundations technically organized as trusts often provided generous compensations to trustees. Usually the compensation is a percentage of income. The fifteen trustees of the Duke Endowment, for example, are each paid a fifteenth part of 3 percent of the annual trust income which, in 1963, amounted to $30,000,[6] a sum which undoubtedly has been increased substantially since that year. Payment of even this relatively munificent sum is entirely in accord with the tradition of trusteeship of charitable funds. By way of contrast, most foundations organized as corporate bodies, provide little or no salary or *per diem* compensation for service. The Ford Foundation, for example, pays each of its trustees the flat sum of 5,000 dollars a year. More recent information on trustee compensation indicates that, among trustee-administered foundations, more than half of the trustees receive under 5,000 dollars, somewhat more than a third receive from 5,000 to 20,000 dollars, and about a fifth enjoy compensation ranging from 20,000 to 50,000 dollars, a few foundations exceeding the latter figure. On the other hand, the two dozen staffed foundations for which recent data became available gave no trustee more than 20,000 dollars and two-thirds of them paid less than 5,000 dollars.[7]

So far as the law is concerned, reasonable fees for trustees are permissible. "The one caveat in all questions of compensation is that fees must be based on the reasonable worth of the service. . . ." [8] Unquestionably, considering the kind of activity in which foundation trustees ought to indulge and the demands that ought to be made on their time and energy, a strong argument could be made for reasonable compensation at least for members of boards of the more mature, intermediate, and general-purpose foundations. The promise of such compensation would make it clear to board members that if they accepted the responsibilities of membership they would have to sacrifice a good deal of time and engage in serious effort. It would fortify the chairman of the board, or his alter ego, in demanding study and thought by board members over protracted periods. Payment might also help to inhibit the practice, which is indulged in often enough in some foundations to constitute a scandal, of a foundation trustee using his position to secure favorable actions on grants for his pet charities or the pet charities of his friends. Since he is guaranteed a formal return for his services, he should be less tempted to seek informal compensation and less able to find moral justification for doing so.

Probably the clinching argument for giving reasonable compensation to board members is that an appeal for service can be made to those individuals in the community who do not normally serve on non-profit boards because they do not enjoy the large salaries, perquisites, or family wealth that most businessmen and others who customarily serve on boards enjoy. Payment to a social-service worker, a minister, or even a college professor is necessary compensation if he is to set aside time and energy for foundation board service.

Against these arguments for compensation, Dr. Young has demonstrated that the prestige associated with service on major foundation boards and the opportunity it offers for service to the nation and community usually are sufficient reward to induce outstanding individuals to serve without compensation. He points especially to the Rockefeller Foundation as one which has never offered compensation but whose board over the years "is a veritable list of men of accomplishment and distinction." [9] The experience of a few large and justly famous foundations is not, however, likely to be duplicated by less well known, but none the less important, foundations, service for which does not offer a cachet like that of service on a Rockefeller board. Nor does the experience of that board necessarily provide a relevant precedent for today's boards. If these are to be socially and intellectually in tune with the times and bridge the so-called "generation gap," they will have to become less exclusive and less "collegial," and to achieve that condition they will undoubtedly have to think twice before denying compensation to members.

*　　*　　*

The writings about boards of trustees of eleemosynary institutions usually provide anything but exhilarating reading. The principal reason is that so much of the literature is concerned with organizational manipulation and administrative procedure. Another reason is that, as personalities, trustees normally conform so closely to type as to defy idiosyncratic, and hence, "human-interest" treatment. Nevertheless, the intrinsic importance of the subject requires attention, especially in the case of foundations. Though a private organization and properly jealous of its autonomy, a foundation exists for the benefit of the public, and the public has a right to know what a foundation is doing, what it plans to do, and how it operates. The public also has a right to be heard and to have a channel of communication to a foundation. Since the law regards the board as the public's representative in a foundation, it should be a principal agency through which the rights of the public are protected and vindicated. If only to discharge this responsibility more effectively, boards need more competent, more dedicated, and more representative personnel, more efficient internal organization, and a greater opportunity to involve themselves in planning a foundation's response to the moral and intellectual challenges of the times.

NOTES—CHAPTER 3

1. Mulreany, "Foundation Trustees—Selection, Duties, and Responsibilities," *UCLA Law Review*, Vol. XIII, No. 4 (May, 1966), p. 1065; also Fremont-Smith, *Foundations and Government* (New York, 1965), pp. 91-111.
2. Embree and Waxman, *The Story of the Julius Rosenwald Fund* (New York, 1949), p. 199.
3. See, for example, Reeves, "The Cool Billions," *The Nation* (April 4, 1966), p. 384.
4. Young and Moore, *Trusteeship and the Management of Foundations* (New York, 1969), pp. 49, 53.
5. Andrews, *Philanthropic Foundations* (New York, 1956), pp. 85-89.
6. See copy of Duke indenture in *Comments on Treasury Report* submitted to Committee on Ways and Means, 89th Cong., 1st Sess., 1965, II, p. 510, and *Hearings* before Subcommittee No. 1 on Foundations, 88th Cong., 2nd Sess., Washington, 1964, p. 299.
7. Zurcher and Dustan, *The Foundation Administrator* (New York, 1972), pp. 100-102.
8. Fremont-Smith, *op. cit.*, p. 154.
9. Young and Moore, *Trusteeship and the Management of Foundations* (New York, 1969), p. 41.

Chapter 4

THE FOUNDATION
ADMINISTRATOR

ONE OF THE MORE startling discoveries a student of foundation administration will make is that there is a relative dearth of professional administrators, who are employed by a foundation and compensated because of their experience as philanthropists or because they possess some skill or expertise useful in carrying out the foundation's administrative and program activities. As we have already noted, most of the small family foundations are controlled and administered by the donor or trustees. Because their philanthropy is devoted to local projects and because the projects are not often changed, the foundations do not appear to require paid professional help. Hence most of them make do with the services of family representatives, an occasional trustee, a consultant or two, and possibly one or two clerical assistants. The same holds for most company-sponsored and community foundations. As with the small family foundation, one or two individuals, who may be trustees, serve without direct compensation as officers of the foundation. Their contribution is supplemented by the paid or unpaid services of banking or corporate officers who handle routine legal, financial, and similar responsibilities.

The staffing is somewhat more complicated for the operations of foundations that have reached what we have called an intermediate level of development. Foundations such as Bush, Duke, Hartford, Houston, Kettering, Kresge, Lilly, Luce, McConnell Clark, A. W. Mellon, R. K. Mellon, Moody, Mott, Olin, Pew, Scaife, and Woodruff—to name some rather well-known ones—each of which has assets of magnitude (some are among the nation's largest) and is quite active, may have as many as seven or eight paid people with some sort of title. Some of them have less than that number and a few have only one or two people. Thus though these quite wealthy foundations may have accepted professional staffing in principle, some of them are still relatively indifferent to the idea and consider a staff of any great size unnecessary. Again the principal reason is the nature of their program which is largely, if not exclusively, of the supportive variety, grants being made to well-known and respected institutions.

Only as we begin to consider the few large and active general-purpose foundations, which tend to eschew conventional supportive grants in favor of more project grants, do we begin to encounter organizations with paid staffs of more than a dozen people. Thus foundations like Rockefeller Brothers, Commonwealth, Danforth, and Kellogg may have program and administrative staffs of fifteen or sixteen people although some are only part-time. In 1968, Kellogg, for example, listed seventeen administrative and program people, and in 1967 it also listed about 35 consultants. The Danforth Foundation employed seventeen staff people in 1968.[1]

Among the very largest and most active of the general-purpose foundations, staff registers begin to climb and there is a chain of command and appropriate hierarchical gradations. Beside the president or executive director, there may be one or more vice presidents and executive associates, program directors, program associates, and other associates and assistants. Officials may even be assigned to at least rudimentary divisions or departments. When staff is added to take charge of internal administration and finance, and supporting clerical personnel for all areas of activity are tallied, the total number of employees becomes modestly impressive.

Soon after it became active the Ford Foundation, the wealthiest and philanthropically the most diversified foundation, had some 230 employees, of whom about 40 were at the decision-making level.[2] Thirteen years later, in 1968, the number of Ford administrative and program staff, including various foreign and field representatives, had increased to a total of 242 and some 20 more were added during the following two years. There was a bureaucratic structure consisting of four principal divisions, namely, "national affairs," "humanities and the arts," "education and research," and "international division."[3]

In 1967 the Rockefeller Foundation had a headquarters staff of some 80 individuals and a field staff comprising about 150. There was probably some duplication of names in the two categories and quite a number of part-time employees and consultants in the field staff.[4] The "organization chart" was comprised of five principal program divisions. In the same year, the Carnegie Corporation listed 23 staff people, although again some were obviously part-time. Early in the 1960s, the Alfred P. Sloan Foundation, a family foundation of the intermediate type that is gradually being transformed into a general-purpose institution, got along with eight people who had a staff title. Today, it has more than doubled the number of full-time program and administrative staff people.

Even for the larger general-purpose foundations data such as these have their limitations as indices of what might be considered normal staff size. Especially is this true in the case of the Ford and Rockefeller foundations which are very large and very active. These two are also partly "operating foundations"; that is, they themselves conduct programs, especially in foreign countries, or they are intimately involved in supervising and counseling programs. "In-house" activities of that kind require relatively large field staffs and somewhat larger staffs in the home office than are required by the purely "grant-making" institution.

It should be added that, besides the small number of wealthy, well-staffed foundations, there are also some foundations, financially of relatively modest size, which carry on substantial "in-house" programs, or programs over which they exercise considerable formal or informal direction, in addition to making grants to others. As a consequence, these may also employ a comparatively large staff. Russell Sage Foundation, for example, with a portfolio of somewhat over 27 million dollars—a portfolio of respectable magnitude though much less than that of other, well-known foundations—has acquired an outstanding reputation as a center of research in the formal and applied social sciences. It employs permanent and temporary staffs often in excess of the number employed by foundations which may have ten times the Russell Sage assets. A somewhat similar observation may be made of the Twentieth Century Fund and of other foundations with "in-house" programs whose assets are only modest in magnitude.

What it comes down to is that foundations employ few people (except for a relatively few, wealthy, general-purpose foundations with both grant-making and internal programs and an even lesser number of well-known foundations with modest assets that have ambitious internal programs). Such staff as does exist, moreover, is unevenly distributed. In a recent study of the foundation administrator, it was found that all the foundations employed a total of some 1400 individuals above the clerical level. Of these, somewhat over a thousand were employed full-time and the remainder part-time. Of the full-time administrators, approximately 25 percent were employed by the Ford Foundation, 15 percent by the Rockefeller Foundation and 12 percent by the Carnegie Corporation and the Commonwealth, Danforth, Duke, Houston, Kellogg, Kettering, R. K. Mellon, Mott, Rockefeller Brothers, and Sloan foundations. The remaining full-time and part-time administrators, approximately 60 percent of the total of 1400, were dispersed among some 332 additional foundations. One hundred seventy-six of these employed only one person either on a full-time or part-time basis and 75 foundations employed two such persons. The following table, borrowed from the study,[5] supplies the appropriate statistics.

NUMBER OF FOUNDATIONS EMPLOYING FULL-TIME AND/OR PART-TIME EXECUTIVE-LEVEL STAFF

Number of Foundations	Ranges of Staff	Total Number of Staff
176	1	176
75	2	150
65	3-5	246
17	6-10	134
10	11-100	233
2	Over 100	422
Total 345		Total 1361

The study also confirmed the observation, made earlier, that many wealthy foundations at the intermediate level of development have no paid staff. Of the 662 foundations studied, those that had no paid staff included 32 foundations with assets between 25 and 100 million dollars, six foundations with assets between 100 million and 300 million dollars, and one foundation with assets between 300 million and 1 billion dollars.

Critics of foundations are fond of suggesting that Professor C. Northcote Parkinson could have derived his famous law quite as successfully by observing the American foundation, as he did by observing the British naval establishment.[6] This brief investigation suggests the contrary. It is of course true that staffing is a function of program rather than of asset size; and that because the great majority of foundations maintain a conventional, over-the-counter, supportive type of program, managerial considerations discourage the employment of staff. On the other hand, even such programs could be improved if at least a minimum of experts were hired. Access to professional help would make possible greater diversification among recipients of grants, more considerate treatment of applicants than is now the rule, more thorough advance investigation and appraisal of projects, and at least some monitoring of projects.

Moreover, if foundations are denied the expertise to guide them in making socially desirable judgments on the allocation of their resources, their philanthropy can hardly be of a pioneering variety. Indeed except for a few foundations that are willing to invest in trained staff to focus brains and imagination on various projects, and to dare to take the initiative in determining how and why their money is to be spent, the foundations' vaunted claim to be trail blazers and risk-bearing enterprises has a somewhat hollow ring.

Occasionally, however, foundations can overdo the matter of staffing. Especially among the few more active and more prominent foundations there is evidence that bureaucracies do indeed have a Parkinsonian tendency to swell to a point where declining real work loads require some artificial stimulants. Some staff people develop a great fondness for airports, air travel, and distant places. Congressional investigating commit-tees, for example, have complained that whenever they seek to reach a foundation official, he is either abroad, or just about to depart, or just about to return. Other foundation administrators may decide that office routine and "homework" are expendable or can be "delegated." As a result, it is diffi-cult to eradicate the impression in the mind of the less sympa-thetic "observers" that foundation personnel are themselves expendable and that Parkinson's law is applicable to foundation work.

Recruitment of personnel by foundations is quite informal. Usually people are hired because they are recommended by an existing staff member or trustee or by persons connected with the donor family or business. Whom one knows is ob-viously important if one wants a foundation job. Occasionally a foundation may proceed to make formal inquiry at universi-ties, banks, management consultant firms, or other foundations, particularly if it is looking for a program or administrative specialist. Normally direct application for a job is not encour-aged although in recent years some of the more forward-looking foundations have not been averse to considering such applications and have occasionally made appointments.

As for training and previous experience, foundations con-tinue to favor candidates who come from academe. Usually the appointees are individuals who have had administrative experience in an educational institution or who have moved from teaching into administration; or they may have been faculty members whose academic specialty is closely related to a new foundation program or grant-making area. Occa-sionally a faculty member may be chosen who has come to the foundation's attention because he served as a consultant or as a member of a foundation sponsored and financed project.

Government, or public service of some kind, is also a popular background for the foundation staff man or woman. In recent years, employees from all levels of government but especially from Washington have been finding their way into the ranks of the private foundation. Those who come from a government agency may find that a few of their new colleagues had previously been identified with some quasi-public body or with some privately sponsored social-welfare or educational agency, or, possibly, with an activity directly or indirectly connected with the United Nations. Quite often staff people with an immediate background of public service may have come originally from the faculty or administrative staff of a university. Preference shown for a public-service background may reflect, in part, the more socially conscious type of foundation program that is currently gaining favor.

Other fields from which recruits may be derived include journalism, the law, and business and finance. The latter are usually tapped for a foundation's internal management and for accounting and investment activities, although, especially in the case of business-sponsored foundations, persons with a business or financial background may assume responsibility for all aspects of foundation activity, including program. Lawyers gravitate into foundation positions, especially top management, often because they were intimately identified with the organization of the foundation and served as counsel both for the foundation and its founder.

Opportunities for promotion are relatively generous among the few foundations with sizable staffs. Even among them, however, the top position is likely to be reserved for an outsider and not given to one coming from the ranks. In selecting the outsider, the foundations show somewhat the same preference as to background that they exhibit in recruiting staff in general. The retired university dean or president, or one who can be persuaded to retire, is the favored candidate. Occasionally someone is chosen who has won his spurs in government or some form of quasi-public service. Several recent appointments suggest there is growing interest in persons coming from the medical and related areas. In the case of foundations with relatively limited staffs, that is, from three to five individuals, the chief executive is often a business man, banker or lawyer who acquired his position for reasons which I have already discussed.

In the period after World War II, American foundations produced some unusually capable administrators and philanthropic leaders. Particularly outstanding were men like Emerson Andrews, Orville Brim, McGeorge Bundy, Evans Clark, John Gardner, J. Steele Gow, McNeil Lowry, William McPeak, Henry Allen Moe, Robert Morison, Marshall Robinson, John Russell, Shepard Stone, and Donald Young. Nevertheless, the random and almost accidental methods used to staff the foundations during that period too often resulted in people being hired who were of rather indifferent caliber as respects both intellectual fibre and the degree of wisdom they brought to their philanthropic assignment.

As respects especially the middle-level "philanthropoid" —to use Frederick Keppel's semantic invention—the portrait of the administrator that emerges is not too reassuring to those who want to attract real talent and build an expert foundation service. The chances are that the composite "philanthropoid" who moved into a foundation during the past two decades is a cut or two above the average of his generation in mental acumen with perhaps a *cum laude* diploma from an Ivy League institution or liberal arts college. He may have majored in science or mathematics, but he is more likely to have majored in one of the social sciences, or their current, semantically newly dignified equivalent, the behavioral sciences. He is highly articulate and fired with zeal, but not a particularly discriminating zeal, to improve the lot of the common man. For that reason he is inclined towards "action" programs or programs that support scholarships or fellowships.

Sometimes he is so impatient to enter the social struggle that he fails to take the time to earn a doctorate or other advanced degree. That fact may color his attitude towards "research." He admires that word and undoubtedly understands its connotations. Nevertheless, having neither the time nor the energy required for bona fide research, he is likely to become a devotee of the kind of "research" that is distilled from the conference-room discussion rather than from the laboratory or from patient library investigation and observation in the field. His kind of research produces results which can be mimeographed and bound in not more than 150 pages or printed quickly in a foundation-subsidized soft-cover edition of which at least two-fifths of the verbiage is devoted to "recommendations."

Nor is he likely to be a systematic worker in his own academic specialty, if he has one. Rather too frequently work in that specialty, as well as his office routine and responsibilities, may fall victim to the peripatetic weakness described earlier, namely trips to institutions that are carrying out some program supported by the foundation, or where his services as commencement or convocation orator are in demand, or where one of the innumerable conferences to which his kind is addicted is being held. As a consequence relatively few foundation staff people muster the personal and professional discipline, or undergo the sustained intellectual labor, necessary to produce a really scholarly book or composition.

In advancing a cause, implicit or explicit in a project which he may recommend, the staff man of one of the better-manned foundations—as distinct from one in a donor-controlled foundation—may occasionally exhibit courage, perhaps more courage than a university professor devoted to the same cause, because the professor, unlike the foundation man, has tenure and cannot be dismissed for his opinions. But even the bravest of foundation staff men will falter in the face of what he regards as "established" opinion, particularly as that may be articulated by the heads of the older and more prestigious foundations, and by committees of the National Academy of Sciences, the Social Science Research Council, the American Council on Education, the American Association for the Advancement of Science, the American Council of Learned Societies, and similar bodies. It is a characteristic that blunts his critical faculty—or provides a substitute for it—in an occupation where the critical faculty is a *sine qua non* of effective service.

Politically, the average foundation staff man is usually left of center if not socialistic in his philosophy and social values. He welcomes government welfare programs and the use of private philanthropic funds to supplement government welfare and other projects. He tends to reject criticism of grants that establish nonprofit enterprises in competition with taxable enterprises (to the dismay of Congressman Patman's subcommittee on small business). He is also likely to be somewhat curt and rather negative with individuals whom he regards as old fogies, with DAR and American Legion patriots, with self-appointed promoters of the "American way of life," with antiquarians who want to preserve the latest among the beds that Washington is suspected to have slept in, and with orthodox businessmen who believe that Coolidge was a great president.

Critics of foundations also occasionally insist that the contemporary foundation administrator is peculiarly liable to certain weaknesses, among them intellectual arrogance and snobbery, and a tendency to treat with condescension, if not contempt, many of those who seek his attention.* As I have said, some administrators also neglect staff work: they allow others, particularly proponents of projects and foundation consultants, to do it for them, but then they assume credit for it. Such weaknesses are the result—so it is alleged—of the staff man's inability to resist the temptations and blandishments that are innate in his position as an administrator of vast funds and a dispenser of patronage.

There is probably more than a grain of truth in these strictures. One of the wisest of foundation executives, the late Edwin Embree, in writing with his associate, Julia Waxman, about the Rosenwald Fund, observed that "officers and trustees, constantly being appealed to and deferred to, can scarcely

---

* I shall comment on this failing again, see pp. 67ff.

avoid an exaggerated idea of their own importance. . . ." [7] It is indeed difficult for an otherwise unassuming young man or woman who becomes a program officer of a wealthy and active foundation five or six years after graduation from college—or for that matter for any foundation executive— to resist the adverse psychological impact of commanding great wealth and arranging for its distribution. The constant red-carpet treatment meted out by hopeful applicants; the deference displayed by the powerful; his acceptance into the power structure of the community and often the nation; the enthusiastic approval with which his intellectual equals or superiors in government, business, and the universities, greet his most inane remarks; such treatment can turn even the wisest and most mature head. A foundation man can develop a decidedly distorted image of himself unless he is even more careful than others invested with power.

Obviously, what is revealed in this "portrait" of the foundation administrator are some qualities that excite admiration, and some that are barely tolerable. As an administrator, he is exposed to the peculiar temptations of his office and unless exceptionally well endowed with a sense of humor directed primarily at himself, he can rather readily progress from youthful arrogance to middleaged fatuousness. As for intellectual capacity the portrait suggests that the representative foundation executive can be equated with the majority of slighly higher than medium-grade college faculties.

The truly ambitious among the foundation administrators often come to realize that there is little professional challenge in most foundation work and that one is seldom goaded towards a higher level of intellectual and professional competence. Except for a half-dozen operating foundations, and a few of the project-oriented foundations, he realizes that foundations and scholarship, and even foundations and intellectual rigor, rarely mix. He inevitably becomes dissatisfied, and the very best may resign and move elsewhere, normally back to the university or perhaps to government. Rather too often those who remain are too old to move or are seduced by the relative security and limited demands of the job; they may be scholars who feel they are "through with research" and want to become "administrators." Younger people who remain may have the real forte of academic "swinger" and verbal public-relations "gladhander" and may find a foundation an entirely comfortable base of operations for such talents.

Over the years, leaders of the more advanced foundations have given sporadic attention to the problem of recruiting more young people of superior quality. Some of these leaders have conducted courses in philanthropy or seminars on foundation behavior at leading universities to inform as many students as possible about the way in which foundations operate. They hoped to attract at least a few to the rank of junior staff. Still others have suggested even more elaborate programs and curricula in the colleges and universities to train potential foundation executives. From time to time, suggestions have also been made that foundations should publicize opportunities for able and eager young people and even provide suitable temporary openings to give young staff candidates a chance to observe foundation work at first hand and become at least temporarily involved in it.

Some of the less ambitious of these suggestions and experiments may deserve support. Basically, however, the problem is not one of specialized training for foundation service. Rather it is the problem of attracting to foundations the best young people. These are the ones who are broadly and liberally trained, who possess imagination and the courage to challenge the status quo, and who have the knowledge and understanding to meet scholars and leaders on their own ground and even themselves contribute to scholarship, social reform and cultural change. Attracting such talent is not likely to succeed, however, unless foundations become more intimately involved than they are at present in designing—and even administering —the projects for which they spend their money. Young people with ambition want to be "where the action is" and be a part of that action. Such young people will demand that a foundation offer more than an opportunity to sit behind a counter and listen to requests for financial support of causes others are sponsoring. They will also want to be a part of the process of deciding in the first instance where the foundation largess is to go, and to have some continuing, professional association with those who spend that largess.

If, therefore, foundations wish to compete effectively with those sectors of our society that attract the more competent youth, as, for example, the universities and the learned professions, they will have to move away from the orthodox, grant-making type of organization towards the operating type of foundation. That does not mean that our great foundations must all become operating foundations; but it does mean that more of them must offer their staffs, or prospective staffs, an opportunity to survey social and intellectual needs, and sometimes, at least, become closely identified with the administration of the projects they decide to finance.

Any such modification of foundation practice will probably provoke criticism that foundations are usurping the role of educational, research, and action agencies in our society. It can indeed reinvoke, in all its traditional bitterness, the academic condemnation of foundations as agencies which "use" universities and load down their budgets with expenditures not appropriate to an educational institution. It can call forth the kind of denunciation not unlike that which universities nowadays direct at government funding agencies when the latter tie administrative strings to the use of public funds or categorize their grants too minutely. A maximum of diplomacy and understanding will be required of foundation administrators to prevent, repel, or mitigate such charges and to make clear that, despite their command of funds, they do not want to monopolize decision-making, but to share it.

In seeking to improve the quality of the young person whom they wish to attract to philanthropy as a career, foundations could also give more attention than they have to the economic rewards. Thanks to the Carnegie Foundation for the Advancement of Teaching, and to those who guide the agencies that provide pensions for academic people which that foundation helped initiate, namely the Teachers Insurance and Annuity Association and the College Retirement Equities Fund, foundation staff members have have been made eligible, along with university professors, for such pensions. As a result, increasingly since 1950, the leading foundations have authorized plans for their respective staffs, most of them of a noncontributory character. During the last decade, moreover, other fringe benefits have been introduced, including group life insurance, medical and hospital insurance, and foundation-financed periodic medical examinations. In respect of customary fringe benefits, certainly among the older and larger foundations, staff people are now doing as well as university people, but there are still a surprising number of foundations that have not progressed much beyond 1915 in this matter.

Foundation management might also improve salaries to raise the quality of staff personnel. Some heads of foundations and those next in command are rather well paid—perhaps too well paid. So, too, are occasional "operating" trustees who are guaranteed a fixed percentage of the income from a trust indenture or have had their fees fixed by a too-generous judge. But the compensation of lesser foundation officers, especially of junior program officers and officers for internal administration, sometimes leaves something to be desired. There is also great variation in salary levels from foundation to foundation. Probably the principal reason for this is the lack of professional standards and ignorance of the "going" rate for particular jobs. Another reason is that foundation heads often desire to emulate university pay standards but fail to realize that during the past two decades, and especially during the 1960s, university salaries and perquisites, including the perquisites of academic moonlighting, have sometimes provided gross incomes for professors and administrators that far exceed the salaries of comparable foundation executives. In any case, salaries are in need of review by those who wish to make foundation service more attractive and to improve foundation administration.

As more foundations pass from the stage of a family-controlled or trustee-dominated fund to that of a mature philanthropic organization with, possibly, some operating responsibilities, and as foundations are required to assume an increasing degree of public accountability, the role of the foundation administrator will change accordingly. Inevitably he will become more visible to the public, and public appraisal of his activity will become more thorough. As these changes come to pass, it is the stature and performance of the administrator, rather than any philosophical argument about the foundation's contribution to cultural and institutional pluralism, that will keep the foundation socially viable and determine whether it will continue to enjoy public acceptance. Breadth and excellence of training and experience, concern for the cultural and technical progress of mankind, capacity to lead and to innovate in seeking to solve intellectual and social problems, and a moral capacity to resist the unique temptations of a foundation post—these are the qualities that the foundation administrator of the future must possess if he is to serve his employer well and if his employer is to have a useful future.

To discover and challenge a corps of such administrators will thus be among the principal tasks, if not the principal task, of those who now manage and direct foundations. To ignore that task, or even to cope with it with less than the highest degree of dedication and understanding, is to court the decline and ultimate extinction of the foundation as an important institution in American society.

NOTES—CHAPTER 4

1. See annual reports of foundations cited for the years in question.
2. MacDonald, *The Ford Foundation—the Men and the Millions* (New York, 1956), p. 96.
3. Ford Foundation, *Annual Report* (1968).
4. Rockefeller Foundation, *President's Review* (1967).
5. Zurcher and Dustan, *The Foundation Administrator* (New York, 1972), pp. 19-36; 20-26.
6. See his *Law and Other Studies in Administration* (Boston, 1957), pp. 7-13.
7. Embree and Waxman, *The Story of the Julius Rosenwald Fund* (New York, 1949), p. 213.

Chapter 5

COMMITTING A FOUNDATION'S RESOURCES

IF THE VENERABLE cliché that "it is harder to give away money than it is to earn it" is correct, a foundation's chief business, which is giving away money, must be difficult indeed. From my own observations, however, a great many foundations— perhaps a majority of them—do not regard the business as being particularly difficult. In many cases, a foundation can dispose of money with the utmost dispatch and with a mini- mum of or even no administrative complications. This is true especially with foundations which pursue a supportive or conduit type of program. I observed such a foundation give away a half-million dollars in less than ten minutes, and 50,000 dollars in less than five minutes. The grants were made to perfectly worthy causes, in one case a hospital, and in the other, a boy's club. This was possible partly because the persons who represented the applicant institutions were long-standing friends of the foundation's founder-donor who made the decision in these two cases with the assurance of the support of his board of trustees.

The manner in which the grants I mentioned above were made is, of course, typical of those normally made by a donor-controlled primitive or intermediate family foundation. The administrative procedure was informal and expeditious, as well, for the donor or trustees of such foundations seldom see any advantage even in investigating applicants to determine the extent of their need or to establish some order of priority for the commitment of a foundation's always scarce resources.

Procedures are quite different when the seasoned, general-purpose foundation, and many of the more mature intermediate foundations, with some professional or quasi-professional staff, dispose of money. The procedures can be a complicated and time-consuming business; and the grants which are recommended or authorized may be the end product of an extended effort on the part of the administration.

If such a foundation is at least partly "operative" which, as I have already noted, is sometimes the case, the staff may initiate and design a project and the foundation may continue close association with the project's operation after it is authorized, sometimes administering it directly. This often happens outside the United States, where the initiative and know-how of the foundation staff, or of expert consultants whom the foundation may have assembled, are deemed necessary if the project is to succeed. In lieu of direct administration, the foundation may seek to persuade a university or comparable institution to sponsor the project and assume legal responsibility for its operation. In such a case, also, the foundation's continued association with the project, although informal, may remain quite close. Much of the most creative philanthropy in America and abroad has been handled in this fashion, and although it presently is quite limited in volume and restricted to a very few foundations, it is likely that the future will see more of it.

Normally, the major foundations make grants at the request of various individuals and institutions that make up the foundation's "customers." They are, of course, usually educational, medical, scientific, welfare, and other enterprises which qualify for philanthropic support. Before they decide on who should be their potential "customers," the more sophisticated foundations first seek to delimit, with some precision, their respective areas of concern or interest. They also determine the type of grant they will make, that is, whether for buildings, endowment, basic equipment, and other "capital" purposes, or strictly for projects of limited duration involving research, experimentation, and demonstration, or for the initiation, advancement, or strengthening of some institution or process.

The decisions that a foundation makes as to its areas of concern obviously affect its role in a society. And proper decisions must be made if a foundation is to be innovative and creative. There are a few foundations that take this responsibility seriously. They go to some lengths to explore and define their role, and to redefine it from time to time. Much staff time may be devoted to this subject and the directors may call on advisors, either unofficial or formally appointed. A classic example of such a study was that made by the Ford Foundation when, at the end of the forties, it began to think seriously about spending the income of the two Ford estates that had come to it. The foundation recruited distinguished educators and other specialists who, under the direction of H. Rowan Gaither, a lawyer and later the foundation's president, consulted with heads of universities and other cultural centers and with other foundations.

Then in November 1949 the Gaither Committee issued an extensive report outlining certain broad areas in which the Committee recommended the foundation become active and these recommendations were subsequently adopted by the foundation.[1] Since that time, Ford, has redefined its areas of concern, at least in part, on several occasions.

As a rule, those who make recommendations about a foundation's future activities try to reflect society's priorities and to expand the opportunities to advance intellectual development and research. Nevertheless, an amazing similarity sometimes may be observed between the areas of concern in which a foundation becomes interested, even after an exploratory and presumably objective review, and the pet social or the academic or professional interests of a new head of a foundation or of some influential member of a foundation's staff. Occasionally, also, there appears to be no difficulty in preserving some program in which an established administrator has a vested interest, however far removed that may be from the foundation's newly established program. It thus becomes difficult, sometimes, to overcome the suspicion that defining or redefining a foundation's area of concern is a process of rationalization and justification rather than one of empirical and objective exploration and analysis. As a consequence, sensitive observers doubt the intellectual integrity of some of the foundation's personnel, and confidence in the foundation itself declines. The really serious loss, of course, as already suggested, is the failure of a seasoned foundation to respond to a society's highest and most intensely felt needs.

Of the projects which are proposed to a foundation, about one in ten is likely to be adopted. The others are declined usually not with the excuse that the foundation is fresh out of money but with the statement that the proposal is outside the foundation's area of concern. And some of the requests for support, it must be conceded, are indeed quite "far out." The procedure observed in giving the proposal which appears to have some promise further consideration varies only slightly among the larger, reasonably well-staffed, general-purpose foundations. What follows is therefore a fair generalization of that procedure.

After the staff man who has received a proposal has decided it comes within the foundation's scheme of things and has some merit, he passes it on for a preliminary staff consideration, during which other staff members may turn it down if the majority does not believe that the proposal merits a second reading. If the proposal survives, someone, normally the staff member who first took up the project, is likely to be assigned the task of "staffing it," a phrase as popular among foundation administrators as among Pentagon colonels. What it means is that the foundation staff man must write an appropriate brief and provide documentation for the proposal so that at a subsequent meeting his confreres can finally make a collective decision whether to go ahead with the proposal or kill it.

In preparing this documentation, the staffer, even if he wished to be as objective as a judge, can scarcely avoid becoming an advocate of the project. By advancing the proposal, he engages in what bears some resemblance to the adversary procedure of an Anglo-American law court. Why he must be cast in this role is not clear, for the procedure has the disadvantage of tempting the staff man to exaggerate the possible merits of the proposal and this, in turn, contributes to the inflated claims about the value of a project of which, from time to time, more than one of the major foundations is guilty. Of course, an occasional staff man can take advantage of this procedure to advance the claims of an institution in which he has a personal interest—as an alumnus, board member, or former employee. Foundations could insure a greater degree of objectivity and, as a consequence, greater certainty as to the relative merits of a proposal if it were assigned at least to two individuals, preferably two who had been trained in different intellectual disciplines or professions.

A decade ago, Dwight MacDonald suggested that the staff

man, in carrying out this major assignment, so surrounded himself with memoranda, briefs of various sorts, and other documents that he becomes quite paralyzed by the sea of paper around him and degenerates into a sort of "leaden Maecenas." [2] The picture was perhaps ever so slightly overdrawn even as respects the executive of the Ford Foundation about whom Mr. MacDonald was writing. To be sure, the flow of type-script into a foundation office about a proposal that is being seriously considered can assume awesome proportions. A major contribution is made by the initiator of the project. However often and however emphatically he may have been cautioned to be sparing of language and succinct in describing the pur-pose for which funds are wanted, any phraseological restraint he may observe is likely to be limited to the letter with which he transmits the description of his project. Usually the latter is a splendid example of what an automatic mimeograph ma-chine can produce if properly goaded.

As the proposal is "processed" it accumulates memoranda galore, especially to convey the wisdom of the foundation's professionals on the subject. Often a staff member suggests the need of additional documentation from the project's pro-ponent, and this request yields further correspondence and memoranda, as does a personal visit to the proponent of the project, if it is undertaken. In many cases, the foundation staff man in charge of the proposal is reminded that there are ex-perts in the universities or elsewhere who might serve as con-sultants in appraising the proposal; and the foundation itself may have regular consultants who may be requested to com-ment on the proposal. Then—an increasingly more common practice in recent years—the staff man may check with other foundations to secure opinions from staff people who may be especially expert in the province of the proposal. Certain it is that by the time the proposal has reached that point in the "grant-making process" where a staff decision is to be taken, the staff man in charge may begin to feel at least somewhat like MacDonald's "leaden Maecenas," or possibly like the sorcerer's apprentice who wonders if he can cope with the paper inundation. Even then, however, the accumulation of paper is not complete; for if the decision at the staff level concerning a project should be favorable, there comes the briefing of the trustees, also chiefly with paper.

If a favorable verdict is given by the trustees, and most projects that advance so far eventually receive a favorable verdict, the foundation head or the program staffer, or both, have the pleasant duty of informing the applicant of his success. This is usually done informally and by the swiftest means of communication available, which is electronic. Thus they savor, at least in a derivative sort of way, one of the principal psychic satisfactions a foundation offers, namely the sense of benevolence that must have been experienced by the Carnegies of history who not only gave away their money but who also earned—or at least accumulated—what they gave away. Saying "yes" is indeed a satisfying experience for a foundation official, and most carry off this pleasant duty with some flair and with no serious criticism from the public.

But alas, as I have noted, about nine times out of ten foundation officials have to say "no" to an applicant either before or after the "grant-making process" has been observed, and neither the way in which foundations come to a negative decision nor the way in which they communicate it to an unsuccessful applicant seems to exhaust a staff man's capacity for tact or diplomacy or require much of his time. Indeed the way in which a foundation comes to a negative decision, and the way it often handles a "customer" to whom it must say "no," has inspired a good deal of criticism of which much is justified.

I well remember the bitterness with which an official of a relatively little-known midwestern university once condemned the whole foundation fraternity after having tried unsuccessfully to arouse some interest in the needs of his institution. Of the hundred or so foundations to which he said he had sent a well-formulated proposal, about twenty-five did him the courtesy of replying. Those foundations that arranged to have one of their staff see him, gave him a "routine thirty minute appointment," and when the thirty minutes had expired, he "was ushered out of the office through means not so devious as to be unnoticeable." He went on to say that he came to realize that "none of the staff people who interviewed him had read his proposal" and that when he came into their august presence, their inevitable greeting was: "tell me all about it." If the interview itself did not end with the staff man's statement that the foundation could not fund the proposal, it was received in the mails shortly thereafter.

Undoubtedly this applicant appealed to some foundations whose areas of concern did not embrace his institution's needs. Admittedly too, foundations are often understaffed, at least for interviewing purposes, and they cannot confer with everyone who demands an audience or study assiduously every presentation before such an interview. At the same time, there was no excuse for the rather flippant treatment this university official received and the treatment which many like him receive. He considered that experience "demeaning," as indeed it was. From first to last the treatment accorded him was an insult to his intelligence and to the institution which he represented. It would appear that foundations calculate to make their public suspicious and condemnatory and to confuse and complicate that public's approach to them.

Arbitrariness is also often manifested by foundations in the procedure they observe in declining a proposal through the mails without any prior interview with the applicant. Far too often a declination of this kind is a form letter or postcard bearing the mimeographed stylus signature of the titled dignitary of lowest grade on the foundation's administrative totem pole. This is sent along, as a matter of bureaucratic routine, to the applicant for support who is to be disappointed. By its very nature, such a communication can offer only the most perfunctory expression of regret, if indeed it offers any; and it cannot, or at any rate does not, provide any reasoned explanation for the declination.

Here, then, is another administrative area in which foundations could improve their behavior. More expert and sympathetic treatment of those who must reconcile themselves to a foundation negative would constitute an admirable expression of administrative sagacity, since the disappointed applicant is likely to become a member of a rather articulate segment of the public—one which feels it has the most reason to complain about foundation policy. In any case, as long as a foundation enjoys tax exemption and is given the status of a quasi-public institution, it has a moral if not a legal obligation to explain why it says "yes" to one applicant for assistance and "no" to another. This should be done even if a policy of being honest requires the foundation man to skirt perilously close to telling the disappointed largess seeker that he and his associates are less capable, or less well-supported institutionally than others who have persuaded the foundation to say "yes." Such reasons for discriminating among applicants, alas, do exist—especially the second—although far less often than foundation executives, prone to favor big-league institutions or scholars with established reputations, are willing to admit. In any event, honesty need not oust tact. Both are virtues; and a greater supply of each of them could be exploited profitably when a foundation says "no."

Considerable improvement could be effected in the "grant-making process" and in the procedure for declining assistance if foundations made serious efforts to improve their communication with the general public. If the members of a foundation made a more sustained and conscientious effort to explain their foundation's *modus operandi* and to describe and delimit the areas in which it will commit funds, those seeking funds could act more efficiently than they do at present; applicants could direct appeals to appropriate, specific foundations and accommodate themselves to each foundation's requirements.

Inappropriate appeals could thereby be reduced and staff time conserved. As well, the foundation staff would not have to deal with so many disappointing conferences or so much correspondence, and when a foundation staff man had to say "no" he might have time to say it gracefully or at least less peremptorily than is customary.

The favored medium of communication with the public is the foundation's published report, issued at various intervals. There was a time not so many years ago when a foundation report was a rarity. The situation has improved somewhat, thanks, in part, to the missionary work of The Foundation Center which, as we have noted, following its creation in the early 1950s, took a strong stand in favor of reports from more foundations than were issuing them at the time. The improvement, though significant, is still relatively limited, and the issuance of public reports remains one of the foundation community's major pieces of unfinished business.

It should be added that the Tax Reform Act of 1969 now requires every foundation with assets in excess of 5,000 dollars to file an annual report. Although only a minimum of information is demanded, and that can be set up in mimeographed form if the foundation wishes, a limited number of copies of the report do have to be filed with certain public officials and the foundation must keep a copy on file at its "principal office" for inspection by the general public and publish a notice of its availability in a local newspaper of respectable circulation.[3] The impact of this requirement is still to be measured but it seems likely to have the effect of persuading a number of foundations that hitherto have been quite secretive about themselves, to issue some kind of report.

However, it is doubtful that the quality of a foundation report has been much improved since those days in the middle fifties when Dwight MacDonald described it as a "literary product that is somewhat more readable than the phone book and somewhat less so than the collected sermons of Henry Ward Beecher."[4] There are quite a number of foundations that do little more than list their grants—a kind of phone book without any sermons and decidedly less useful than either. The more sophisticated foundation, however, may go to the other extreme and describe projects which it currently holds in high esteem in detail, with considerable use of superlatives and a virtual absence of qualificatory phrases or clauses. Rarely, in all cases, is a conscientious effort made to outline the areas of concern or to explain how and why current projects fit into those areas of concern. Usually, indeed, it may be discerned from the reports that some grants which the foundation has made do not fit into any formally announced area of concern, for the extent to which they fail to do so is inversely proportional to the intensity of the effort made to persuade the reader that they do—unless, of course, maverick grants are ignored altogether and simply tabulated. Occasionally the report is exploited to editorialize on the troubles or problems of the times. The editorials may have little relevance to the foundation's programs, though they clearly establish the kinship of the report with the Reverend Beecher's sermons. In far too many reports, as well, are fulsome paragraphs about the founder's philanthropic and business philosophy, or that of some trustee, most of it synthetic and complacently self-serving, and none of it helpful to anyone seeking information about the foundation's program.

To create such documents, foundation information and public-relations officers often have to sacrifice reportorial integrity and smother incipient literary skills, if they have any, and resort to a kind of Aesopian language that would make a Communist dialectician blush. If the end result of their effort is not exactly the rather remarkable literary product described by Mr. MacDonald, it is still remarkable enough—a hybrid of the arts of those who wish to inform, of those who wish to impress, and of those who wish to delude.

Hence many foundation reports do not enlighten the public; they confuse it. Instead of facilitating what we have called the "grant-making process," a report is likely to complicate and obstruct that process. Clearly if such a document is to be something more than a mediocre public-relations effusion, and is to inform those who are thinking about making applications for support, at least minimal efforts will have to be made to improve the report's substance. Among the first such efforts should be the task, described earlier, of defining and illustrating areas of concern. Should this be done, there will probably be fewer requests that the foundation cannot entertain; and perhaps the foundation itself will not have to chronicle too many of its own violations of its areas of concern when it issues a report. Second, the report should be made somewhat more honest than the majority of those currently being issued. For example, it is simply not honest to suggest that a small, endowed, midwestern church-related college is likely to be given the same consideration as an applicant for support as a great Eastern university. Such a degree of candor might make some of the public indignant, but it might lessen the extent of public indignation existing at present.

After all, people do understand that, by the very nature of their mission and because their resources are relatively limited, foundations must discriminate among applicants for their largess. Not even the most hostile critic would deny that they must do so. But because they must discriminate they have a special obligation to explain to the public as honestly and as fully as possible who gets what and why. Were they to do this, they would not only improve their public relations but they would expedite their business of giving away money and make that business administratively more acceptable.

NOTES—CHAPTER 5

1. See *Report of the Study for The Ford Foundation on Policy and Program* (Detroit, Michigan), 1949.
2. MacDonald, *op. cit.*, p. 103.
3. See Tax Reform Act, Sections 101 (d) and 101 (e); Code, Sections 6056 and 6104 (d).
4. *Op. cit.*, p. 101.

Chapter 6

MEASURING THE SUCCESS
OF A FOUNDATION GRANT

SOME OF THE MORE conscientious businessmen who become involved with foundations, as either a donor or trustee, confess
to many frustrations. Most important, they cannot discover
objective criteria for measuring the success of a foundation's
grants. Moreover, most foundation staffs are relatively uncon-
cerned about the matter. I recall that this was a source of
frequent complaint by the founder of the Alfred P. Sloan
Foundation. As one of the creators of General Motors, and for
many years its chief executive, Mr. Sloan was accustomed to

seeing a profit-and-loss statement each year for the company. Mr. Sloan pointed out that there was not even the most rudimentary yardstick for measuring foundation accomplishment or failure. He was not averse to adding that foundation staffs knew how to spend money but had no way of knowing whether the money they spent yielded a return. Implicit in that observation was the unspoken corollary that foundation executives, by and large, were indifferent to the problem of measuring returns on investment and were wasteful and inefficient in the stewardship of resources committed to their care.

Some members of Congress also found this out during hearings on the Tax Reform Act of 1969. As a result, provisions were incorporated in the Act under which foundations will be required to assume "expenditure responsibility" for certain limited types of grants.[1] The foundations must "establish adequate procedures" to see that the proceeds of the grants are spent for the purpose for which the grant was made and obtain full and complete reports from the recipient of the grant. Failure to assume or discharge satisfactorily such "expenditure responsibility" can result in the levying of special taxes on both the foundation and the responsible foundation executive.*

Clearly an elementary requirement of foundation administration should be that of devising procedures to provide "feedback" from the individuals and activities which foundations subsidize and estimate what, if anything, has been accomplished with their funds. Unless such efforts are made, and made systematically, it is impossible to determine whether a grant has attained its professed objectives and whether it should be renewed. It would also be difficult, if not impossible, to inform the public or appropriate government agencies as to just what is being done with funds that enjoy tax exemption.[2]

* For further comment, see pp. 150-151.

Nevertheless, few of those who administer foundations appear to be concerned with this problem of measurement. Instead they are too often satisfied to indulge in a thinly disguised form of public relations to reassure a critic on the foundation board or some other critic of a grant. The public reputation of the recipient of a grant, which may be a famous university or a medical center, is invoked to justify the merit of the decision the board made to spend money, or the staff man may invoke the name and reputation of an individual scholar who receives grants, perhaps by pointing to the number of articles which the researcher has produced with the aid of his subvention. Little if any mention is made of the intrinsic merit of the research delineated in the articles or of the contribution of that research to the particular discipline, or whether the research turned up negative or positive results, either of which may be considered a "success" or a "failure," depending on how the research was conducted and who conducted it. The staff member appears only to wish to create the absurd impression that there are no foundation projects which have failed; there are only projects which may have been more successful than others. Such an approach reduces appraisal and measurement to a farce.

The lack of any commitment to evaluate grants and the desire to substitute public relations for serious investigation only partly explain the lack of progress in measuring grant productivity. Actually it is extremely difficult to develop and apply yardsticks. Values which can be measured in the marketplace are mainly quantitative and statistical, but the values involved in grants to education, science, and the arts, the usual objectives of grants among the older and more sophisticated foundations, do not lend themselves readily to quantitative and statistical measurements. The values affected by such grants are likely to be qualitative in nature, and judgment about them will be subjective. Judgment also requires specialized knowledge of the subject or institution which is being supported. In these circumstances, quantitative analysis, unless used judiciously and perhaps merely to supplement other forms of appraisal, can only distort and mislead.

For example, if a foundation supplements the existing resources of a university or of a medical school with a sizable, but noncategorical grant, how does one measure the additional impetus towards excellence which such a grant made possible? In such a situation the usefulness of quantitative yardsticks is negligible. They are of little value also if one were to measure the productivity of, say, a grant to extend viral research on cancer in animals, especially if all results are inconclusive. Indeed, how is it possible to measure the value of any research if the researcher, quite properly, insists that the research, whatever its outcome, has contributed to knowledge? How especially shall this be done in a politico-social environment where the general public does not understand—and is unsympathetic when it does not understand—the research temper and the ideal of knowledge as an end in itself?

It is also difficult to measure the productivity of grants made to individuals. Chances are that the usual indices of potential ability were used in selecting a recipient and that, in due course, he gave a good account of himself. He may have become unusually creative. He may even have become a Nobel laureate. Presumably the prizes awarded him, his research discoveries, and the books he may have written are objective indications of accomplishments and the foundation staff, being human, are likely to credit themselves with unusual powers of discernment as to potential talent and regard their grant as assistance at a crucial period in the development of the recipient. Nevertheless, how much of the success story was due to the grantee's innate ability, industry, and capacity for concentration, and how much to the foundation's special assistance is a question which would require more than the fabled judicial virtuosity of a Solomon to answer. Or, if a foundation instead of having its money ride with the most qualified candidate, which is usual, had been courageous

enough to divert its support to candidates with only a modest
I.Q., how would one explain the improvement in competence
that might take place? Was it really due partly or wholly to
the grant?

Difficulties in measuring the productivity of a grant are
thus real enough. Nevertheless foundation administrators have
an obligation to their own organization and to the public
to make every effort to develop useful procedures for
appraisal.

In the case of some grants, this should not be too difficult. Follow-up on a capital grant to construct facilities
needs little more than the usual auditing of actual expenditures
by an "outside" agency and a brief review by a foundation
financial officer to determine whether the donee has complied
with the specifications and conditions to which he agreed
when the grant was made. Some foundations go farther than
this and provide a liaison man with the grantee institution to
check on delays and possible wasteful building and installation
procedures.

When a foundation moves from grants for capital expenditure into the realm of grants to support individuals and
institutions, it faces a more complicated task if it wishes to
take stock of what its money produces. As I hinted earlier,
objective measurement of such grants is difficult even though
a plethora of statistics may be available. Direct reports from
those aided must be required and the opinion of third parties
familiar with the recipient individual or institution—teachers,
professors, students, professional colleagues, reviewers, administrative officers, and the like—must be sought. Nor is it
inappropriate for the foundation to use its own staff and consultants as appraisers. Presumably their first loyalty is to the
foundation and its aims, and their opinions can counter any
tendency of third parties to give students and professional
colleagues the benefit of any doubt or even to league themselves with the beneficiaries against the foundation.

But whether reliance is placed on outsiders or on staff,

differences of opinion are inevitable. I well remember that two informed faculty members gave conflicting testimony about a generous grant which a foundation had made to their university to extend and modernize an area of its general curriculum. One asserted that the foundation grant, directly, and by encouraging other givers, had been of the greatest value in opening up new vistas in teaching and research. The other held that the money had done little more than help the university to hire one or two new staff members in understaffed departments and questioned the judgment of the general-purpose foundation in using its relatively scarce resources for such conventional supportive purposes. The foundation will, therefore, have to reconcile itself to the probability the judgment will be clouded by the prejudices or rivalries of those whose testimony it seeks. Above all, it will have to reconcile itself to the fact that everyone's judgment is subjective. Its aim must therefore be to secure diverse opinions and to select those as appraisers who are most knowledgeable and whose opinions are least likely to be influenced by personal considerations or by professional "cronyism."

When foundation philanthropic activity reaches the more sophisticated realm of "project grants" that are characteristic of the older and more prestigious foundations, taking inventory of results probably presents the greatest difficulty. The judgments, on which measurement in this realm depend, often must be based on substantive expertise that a foundation program executive does not possess. To a considerable extent, therefore, the foundation must rely on others who command such expertise. Especially is this likely in the case of projects in scientific, technological, and medical research and, for that matter, in almost any specialized discipline, technology, practice, or profession. Again the problem is to find consultants who are sufficiently immune to the blandishments of professional colleagueship and "cronyism" to be able to give relatively unbiased judgments.

For some kinds of projects, for example, those which provide a prototype of an educational, administrative, or statistical procedure or the design of a fairly sophisticated research project in one of the social sciences, a foundation would be well advised to avail itself of a model for evaluating the activity if one exists, and adapting the model to its needs. Such models—often of a high degree of sophistication—are being developed in some number in such areas as elementary and secondary education, social welfare administration, and econometrics.[3]

Various organizations also offer the kind of expertise which foundations could exploit in an effort to elevate their reportorial and evaluatory responsibilities, as respects projects, to a more professional level. Among them are commercial and nonprofit educational testing services, educational development institutes, nonprofit research organizations, economic and consumer survey centers, management consultant firms, public opinion polling centers, and even research foundations. Russell Sage Foundation, Twentieth Century Fund, Brookings Institution, and the National Bureau of Economic Research, offer relevant talent and experience that could assist grant-making foundations in designing and appraising projects. Existing research models and agencies are not relied on because most foundation administrators do not know that they exist or fail to grasp their relevance to their problems; or they are not encouraged to investigate and use them.

To sum up, it must be reiterated that no existing techniques or procedures, or any combination of them, will produce a wholly satisfactory system of appraisal and feedback for a foundation's grants. Even so, if the techniques and procedures that are available were applied by foundations, they would produce a vast improvement in the accuracy of the evaluations. But there must also be a greater concern for evaluation. Especially must there be a commitment by foundation officials to the expenditure of thought, energy, and funds to insure review and appraisal. More specifically, foundations ought to insist on the following: first, systematic reporting by the recipients of grants, including regular financial reports to be reviewed by the appropriate foundation officers; second, assigning staff members on a full-time basis to the work of appraisal or, what is probably more efficient administratively, assigning that duty to the executive who has recommended the grant and who presumably will have relevant expertise to appraise it; third, employing consultants whose specialties cover all of the foundation's activities and using their services regularly, both in helping to judge the promise of a project before it is approved and in surveying and reporting on its operation after it is approved.

Offering such a prescription for improving the evaluation of projects would be an exercise in the obvious were it not for the fact that so few foundations apply it. Nor are they likely to do so unless and until (as I suggested earlier) the major grant-making foundations become more intimately involved than they have been in initiating and designing a project. At least they will then be forced to hire the kind of staff who will undertake such responsibilities and who will possess the degree of intellectual curiosity and professional competence that will compel them to stay with a project and observe and assess its operation.

In our concern for improving the monitoring of projects, it is well to recall the other side of the problem, which is project autonomy. Foundation officials normally do not need to be reminded that to monitor their grants more effectively, they must move with great care. Otherwise they are likely to jeopardize the autonomy of the recipient of their money and, in doing so, limit his professional independence and possibly endanger the integrity of the project. How easily the two objectives of project accountability and project autonomy can be made to interfere with each other is revealed in the case of grants from government sources. Because of bureaucratic tradition and legislative requirements, the government donor is usually compelled to demand frequent reports from those who receive government funds. They often complain bitterly that such a report is sometimes required to be submitted before they have even begun the funded project but extensions of the grants nevertheless are determined by the amount of "glow" engendered by what obviously must be the reporting of nonexistent accomplishments. Further, it pressures the researcher to develop the arts of public relations and sycophancy and to become a fund raiser rather than a researcher—unless he retires from the field in disgust. To protect both sides requires of a foundation executive a unique degree of sensitivity about the nuances of philanthropy, as well as a capacity on the part of a recipient of a grant to respond imaginatively and creatively to the accounting requirements of foundation stewardship.

NOTES—CHAPTER 6

1. See *Report of the Committee on Ways and Means* to accompany H.R. 13270, 91st Cong., 1st Sess., Aug. 2, 1969, Washington, Government Printing Office, 1969, p. 35; Tax Reform Act of 1969, Act Section 101 (b) and Tax Code Section 4945. For additional discussion on the kind of grants that involve expenditure responsibility by a foundation and the procedures required in monitoring and reporting such grants, see Troyer, "Restrictions on Investment and Program Activities," in *Foundations and the Tax Reform Act of 1969* (Foundation Center, New York), 1970, p. 24.
2. See, generally, relevant discussion on foundation "follow-up" procedures, including the remarks of F. Emerson Andrews and the author, in *Proceedings*, Fifth Meeting of the Advisory Committee for Economic and Statistical Studies of

Science and Technology, sponsored by the Office of Economic and Statistical Studies of the National Science Foundation (Washington, April 5, 1963), pp. 280 ff.

3. See for example, a recent Russell Sage volume by Edward A. Suchman, *Evaluation Research: Principles and Practice in Public Service and Social Action Programs* (New York, 1967).

Chapter 7

THE FOUNDATION'S FINANCES

IT IS DIFFICULT to arrive at a satisfactory estimate of the wealth of all foundations. In 1961, when Professor Ralph L. Nelson was gathering data for his volume on the investment policies of foundations, he estimated that the wealth of all foundations had reached levels between 15 and 17 billion dollars.[1] Five years later, when The Foundation Center collected its data for the third edition of *The Foundation Directory*, it estimated that foundation wealth had reached a total of 20 billion dollars.[2] The fourth edition of *The Directory*, issued at the end of 1971, puts the wealth of foundations at 25 billion dollars.[3]

Estimates such as these are valuable but they must be used with caution. For one thing, it is difficult to achieve an even relatively accurate estimate of the wealth of all foundations because many of them follow the practice of maintaining ledger or acquisition values for their portfolio which are quite out of line with market quotations. Moreover, probably a third of all foundation assets consist of direct ownership of businesses, royalties, and real estate, all of which are difficult to appraise. Then, too, like any computation of wealth, one of foundation wealth can fluctuate considerably. The bear and "mixed" markets of 1969 to 1971 have, no doubt, caused the total worth of foundations to change rather drastically from time to time.

For our purposes, I shall regard 25 billion dollars as a generous estimate of foundation wealth. In an absolute sense, such a sum is impressive, but when it is compared to the wealth of other charitable institutions in the United States, it is a relatively modest sum. Economists estimate that the real property of all privately governed, tax-exempt bodies may total as much as 170 billion dollars.[4] That estimate, of course, does not include the possibly greater aggregate of wealth charitable bodies hold—their business investments, stocks, bonds, royalties, and the like—that provide exempt income. When, moreover, the wealth of foundations is measured against the total national wealth, it seems even more modest. In his study to which I referred, Professor Nelson concluded that, at least during the early sixties, foundations held only 0.75 percent of all financial assets in the United States.[5] Hence though the percentage of all foundation wealth held by only a few foundations may justify some raised eyebrows, the totality of foundation wealth within the national economy is not of such proportions as to support the notion that the foundations have a possible stranglehold on that economy that is occasionally suggested by some social critics and politicians.

The concentration of wealth in a relatively few intermediate, general-purpose, community and business-sponsored foundations, to which I have just alluded, is of course, characteristic of the foundation world. In recent years the Ford Foundation, with assets approximating 3 billion dollars, held about one-eighth of the estimated total of 25 billion dollars. Twelve foundation boards, including that of Ford, controlled somewhat less than one-third of all foundation assets.[6] In its third edition, The Foundation Directory had indicated that some 237 foundations, or 1.2 percent of the total, controlled three-fourths of all assets, the remaining 98.8 percent of all foundations accounting for the other fourth.[7] In taking stock as of 1971, the fourth edition of The Directory indicates that virtually all of the 25 billion dollars attributed to the 26,000 foundations in existence is concentrated in the 5,454 foundations which it lists. "The remaining more than 20,000," says this edition, "are small all of them together relatively negligible in terms of fixed assets. . . ."[8] Foundations thus resemble American business in that there exists a high degree of asset concentration among a relatively few giants. It is not surprising, therefore, that charges of dominance and control of philanthropic policy are directed at some foundations not unlike the charges of monopoly and market control that are directed at big business from time to time.

There are many issues of law and policy that affect the management of a foundation's finances. In the pages which follow, we shall explore four of these issues in some detail.

The first, one that usually enjoys priority in any discussion of foundation financial management, is the issue of diversifying a foundation's holdings. Families that endow foundations usually use large blocks of stock in the corporation on which the family grew wealthy or some other kind of specialized family wealth. Traditionally, concentration of family stock or other assets in a foundation has been tolerated as an inevitable consequence of the policy of encouraging the establishment of foundations. During the past two decades, however, Treasury and congressional investigations, and private studies, have documented abuses that can arise from such policies, and these have led to demands for reform. In some instances the concentration is great enough to give a foundation control of a business; and this has sometimes led the trustees to exploit the foundation as an instrument of business policy and even as an instrument of private gain; philanthropy is accordingly largely forgotten. The temptation to do this has been especially strong when representatives of the founding family, or individuals closely allied with it, have served simultaneously as trustees of the foundation and directors of the controlled business.

Short of this kind of abuse, the concentration of foundation assets in a family business may have undesirable consequences for both the management of the foundation and for its philanthropic policy. More than one foundation board has been divided over policies that could affect the welfare of the controlled business, and the resulting struggle has hardly benefitted the foundation. As for the foundation's philanthropy, one of the more serious possible adverse consequences is a reduction in the volume of the foundation's donations. In order to promote the growth of the family business, or to insure certain tax advantages, or for both reasons, the earnings of the business may be reinvested or, at any rate, not paid out in any reasonable volume. The resulting reduction in the foundation's income necessitates cutting down on its payments to charity. Hopefully the new payout provisions of the Tax Reform Act will prevent this in the future—at least in part.

Another possible adverse effect on the foundation's philanthropy is the restraint which a sacrosanct family holding imposes on the efforts of the foundation trustees to act without limitation in mobilizing the volume and type of assets required to discharge the foundation's current obligations and to fund possible long-term commitments. The trustees might, for example, be discouraged from investing in short-term debt securities to cover current obligations and in bonds to fund commitments beyond a year. When the concentration of family stock discourages this kind of portfolio movement, the result could very well be to reduce the number of long-term projects which the foundation's management might otherwise wish to fund.

Still a third possible adverse consequence of retaining a large block of family stock or other form of family wealth, is that the trustees' freedom to pursue what they regard as an optimum investment policy is limited. In addition to the restraint they feel in making investments best calculated to fund the foundation's existing commitments, they are not free to make decisions to maximize income, or the growth of the portfolio.

Despite these potentially adverse effects of keeping heavy family holdings in foundations, and the criticisms which these holdings have inspired, few foundations have voluntarily pursued, with any vigor, a policy of reducing the holdings. To be sure, Professor Nelson found that diversification is usually farther along among the older foundations than among the others.[9] Nevertheless, few of the large, well-established foundations which he studied had really made significant progress toward diversification. Thus for each of twelve of the 45 foundations which responded to his questionnaire, the largest single stockholding was at least 75 percent of the total portfolio of the foundation. For each of eleven other foundations, it was between 50 and 75 percent. His analysis prompted Professor Nelson to conclude that only one in four of the major, well-established, family-derived, foundations could be classified as "widely diversified" in its stock and security holdings.[10] (It should be noted that the percentages cited are percentages of foundation portfolio values, not percentages of the outstanding stock of the companies in which the foundation has invested. Hence the percentages may or may not mean that the foundation controls the companies in which it holds the stock.)

Case studies of instances when certain of the larger foundations tried to diversify confirm the view that such efforts are not usually pursued with gusto. Thus for some time the Ford Foundation has engaged in rather well-publicized efforts to dispose of some of its original mountain of Ford Motor Company stock. The foundation has even engaged in "swapping" arrangements with other foundations that had a large block of a particular issue other than stock of the Ford Motor Company. After 1955, when this program of divestiture began, the percentage of Ford stock owned by the foundation did indeed decline. Nevertheless, some ten years later, Ford stock still accounted for 57 percent of total foundation assets.[11] At the end of 1968, Ford stock, valued at 1.231 billion dollars, continued to account for about 42 percent of all Ford Foundation assets at market. Moreover, this estimate was probably slightly lower than it should have been, since the price of Ford stock used in the computation was 14 dollars less per share than the quotation for regular Ford voting shares on the exchanges.[12]

Similarly, the Sloan Foundation holds a relatively large block of the original stock in General Motors that the founder and his wife gave it, although from time to time, it also has made an effort to reduce its large volume of this stock. In that foundation's earlier years, more than 80 percent of its then largely equity portfolio was in GM stock. Following major accretions of stock from Mrs. Sloan's estate upon her death in 1956, additional gifts from Mr. Sloan at about the same time, and the transfer to the foundation of still more GM stock following Mr. Sloan's death in 1966, the foundation made sizable disposals of its holdings, including at least one secondary offering through an underwriter in New York. Even so, at the end of 1968, Sloan Foundation holdings of GM stock, valued at 121.9 million dollars, still accounted for more than 45 percent of the foundation's equity portfolio, and for more than 37 percent of the value of the foundation's total securities portfolio.[13]

The examples of the Ford and Sloan foundations could be duplicated by many, if not most, family foundations with considerable assets. They can be duplicated by foundations much older than Ford or Sloan. The Rockefeller Foundation, oldest among the very large, general-purpose foundations, still has a noticeably high concentration of the stock of companies that are directly or indirectly derived from the Standard Oil parent.[14]

Aside from the desire to protect and promote the family business which is perhaps not as uncommon a motive among even some of the larger foundations as most of them insist it is—the considerations which keep trustees from disposing of original stock or other property are numerous and varied. In the first place, as noted earlier, the founding instrument of a foundation may prohibit disposition of the original investment and may even require that future investments be in the same company stock. The classic illustration is the trust instrument of the Duke Endowment which requires the trustees to lend to, or invest in, the Duke Power Company, the "family concern."

Even when there is no legal obstacle to unloading family assets, foundation trustees sometimes hesitate to do so for fear that they might be considered disloyal to the founder or to the founder's family company. This feeling can be especially strong among trustees who have known the donor or are of his generation. To sell the family stock under these circumstances, especially when the stock is profitable—possibly even more profitable than much of the rest of the foundation's portfolio—requires a decision which many such trustees are subjectively incapable of making. The founder of the Sloan Foundation, for example, was wont to express to his fellow trustees on every suitable occasion his confidence in the prospects of GM stock and his opinion, which inevitably followed, that getting rid of the stock—the "family stock" in this case—would not be in the best interest of the foundation. Even the most independently minded and financially sophisticated trustee dislikes to disregard an opinion from such a source.

There are also financial and administrative considerations that discourage trustees from reducing the founding family's stock. Disposing of large blocks of stock on the exchanges is always difficult. The depressing effect on price must be a matter of concern to trustees at any time and never more so than when the stock is that of a founder of the corporation or of an early investor. In addition it is always possible, if not probable, that the investing public, not privy to the considerations which prompt a foundation to sell the family stock and to diversify, may interpret such action as lack of confidence in the family company. When "outsiders" make such a suggestion and raise the issue of confidence, it is serious enough; when it is presumptively raised by friends and associates of one who may have been a founder of the company or one of its guiding lights, it is serious indeed.

It is thus not too difficult to explain, or even to justify, the hesitation of the trustees of a foundation to dispose of family stock and diversify the foundation's portfolio. In any case, partly because a number of foundations have pursued the process of diversification too sedately, but chiefly because a few foundations have exploited the family stock position for nonphilanthropic ends, Congress, in 1969, decided to take a hand and encourage the trustees to diversify. In developing the Tax Reform Act of that year it sought to limit directly the ownership of stock or other assets of a business to prevent a foundation from controlling the business. This the law was to do by establishing a maximum of permissible ownership in any business except one which was clearly related to the foundation's purposes for which it was granted exemption and which was essential to carrying out those purposes. The law sought to establish an ideal maximum of 20 percent of the total amount of a company's voting stock that a foundation might hold. That amount, however, must be reduced by the percentage of the voting stock in the same company owned by any group of so-called "disqualified persons," that is, the donor, his family, foundation executives and trustees, significant contributors to the foundation, and other persons and institutions intimately associated with the foundation. A *de minimis* rule allows a foundation to retain not more than 2 percent of the voting stock of a company without regard to the 20 percent maximum. For holdings in nonincorporated businesses, Treasury regulations were to establish a similar policy. A period of ten years was to be allowed for the disposition of excess stock ownership, and the value of any excess holdings at the end of that period will be taxed at the annual rate of 5 percent with a penalty tax of 200 percent of the value of the excess if the foundation does not thereafter divest within a prescribed minimum period.

Qualifications and exceptions were then introduced into the legislation which made this attempt to establish a 20 percent maximum largely meaningless. The law allows a foundation and "disqualified persons" to own as much as 35 percent of a company's outstanding voting stock if the Treasury agrees that effective control of the company is in the hands of "third parties" unrelated to the foundation. Moreover, if it could be shown that a foundation and "disqualified persons" held not more than 50 percent of the outstanding voting stock of any company on May 26, 1969, at the time this revenue legislation was born, the foundation would be allowed to continue to hold that amount indefinitely, although the holdings could not be increased. The trustees could take as long as 15 years to dispose of any stock in excess of the 50 percent maximum if the existing holdings on May 26, 1969 were more than 75 percent but not in excess of 95 percent of the company's voting stock, and as long as twenty years to dispose of any stock in excess of the 50 percent maximum if the existing holdings fell between 95 percent and 100 percent of the company's voting stock. Finally, if the provisions of the Tax Reform Act ran counter to the requirements of a foundation's charter or trust document that investments be confined to a particular company, the grace period was further extended. The extensions equalled whatever time it might take to conduct a judicial proceeding instituted by the foundation to bring its charter, or other creating instrument, into line with the provisions of the divestiture legislation.[15]

What all this means is that, during the next ten to twenty years, any foundation which, on May 26, 1969, owned (with associated individuals) more than 50 percent of the family business will have to dispose of that excess stock and bring its holdings, together with those of "associates," down to the allowed maximum of 50 percent. If the foundation and associated persons owned less than 50 percent on May 26, 1969, they will be permitted to continue to hold that stock but not to increase it. If additional family stock is given to a foundation in the future, the foundation will have to dispose of it within a prescribed grace period in order to maintain the legally permissible maximum.

Most of the "bite" has thus been taken out of the law as it was originally proposed. During the next decade foundations undoubtedly will unload some family stock and at a more rapid rate than they have in the past. But because foundations still are permitted to hold large blocks of a stock, this new legislation has obviously not eliminated the phenomenon of a foundation-controlled family business. At any rate, it has not removed the temptation to control; and it is unlikely to speed up diversification appreciably from the sedate pace, mentioned earlier.

Even if this legislation had "teeth," it would in no way affect concentrated foundation holdings in family (or any other) stock so long as the amount did not exceed the legal definition of "control." Fifty, sixty, or even one hundred percent of the equity portfolio of a foundation can continue to be in the issue of a single corporation so long as that amount does not exceed the permissible maximum percentage of the entire voting stock of that corporation. It therefore remains quite possible for large foundations to concentrate holdings in "family" oil, automotive, electronic, or other stocks and come nowhere near the impermissible maximum that the law says spells control.

Clearly an effective legal sanction for diversification is still to be attained.

A second issue affecting the stewardship of foundation resources, which has inspired extensive debate and some recent legislation, concerns the relative generosity of a foundation's payments to charitable users. Foundations have been paying out about 1.5 billion dollars a year. If the adequacy of this payout were to be measured by the return on investments enjoyed by institutional constituencies such as pension or mutual funds, total foundation grants clearly ought to be greater. The comment, of course, applies to the foundation world as a whole. It may not be true of individual foundations, especially the older project-oriented foundations, which often have a very high payout, using not only income but some of their principal.[16]

In any event there is no doubt that many a foundation's return to charity could be greater than it is if certain practices which militate against a higher payout were discouraged or eliminated. One of these, as we have already noted, is failure of a foundation-controlled business to pay out earnings and thus reduce the foundation's contribution to charity. Another is foundation investment in assets that are currently unproductive, for example in unimproved land or in growth stocks. Again a foundation, especially one of the smaller ones, may accumulate income and then invest it or hold for distribution later (at least this was true in the past). All such practices either prevent or reduce a current return to chariy.

In his study of foundation investment policies, Professor Nelson documented one of these reasons for a low payout, that of investing in growth stocks or in property which promises appreciation, rather than in assets, such as debt securities, which promise a constant and fairly generous return. Of the 24 large foundations which Professor Nelson once questioned on this point, three identified capital growth as the first consideration of their investment policy; 12 indicated that maximum income was the prime consideration; and six said they sought a balance between the two objectives.[17] Obviously the trustees and investment counsellors of some of these foundations did not consider the maximization of current payout to charitable users a primary obligation.

In 1950, Congress authorized the Treasury to prevent foundations from accumulating investment income, and forced foundations to distribute most of their investment income to charity on a current basis.[18] To some extent this worked, but somewhat more imaginative regulatory legislation was required; and the opportunity to provide it came with the Tax Reform Act of 1969. When, however, Congress began to draft this legislation, some additional ideas about what Congress should do to maximize payout to charity had been thrown into the hopper. Among them were Congressman Patman's suggestions that a foundation should pay out all realized capital gains, both short-term and long-term, and that it should also pay out the contributions it receives instead of adding them to its corpus. There was also the suggestion, the germ of which had been provided by the Treasury in the early fifties, that a kind of "capital levy" be made annually on foundations, especially on those which paid out virtually no income from their investments. The most radical of all the suggestions receiving attention at the time was to limit the life of foundations and to make them plan their payouts to charity in anticipation of the eventual liquidation of all their assets. Early in the sixties Congressman Patman had suggested twenty-five years as the appropriate life span of a foundation; and when the draft of the Tax Reform Act came before the Senate Finance Committee, a sizable number of the Committee proposed an amendment which would have brought the tax exemption of all existing foundations to an end within forty years, and of all new foundations as well.

Decision on this last suggestion was bound to influence

the willingness of foundations to pay out their income. On the one hand, if a foundation's life were to be terminated within a relatively short time, those responsible for investing its corpus logically would seek a maximum immediate return on the investment. Moreover, a foundation facing termination probably would pay to charity most of its realized capital gains and perhaps even the contributions that might come to it. One under sentence of death normally does not hoard wealth even when the death is to be a lingering one. On the other hand, if a foundation were to continue in perpetuity, obviously the directors must make some effort to secure appreciation of its investments, even at the expense of immediate grants for projects. Nor could it afford to grant to charitable users the contributions which might have been made to it.

The "death sentence" amendment was eventually dropped from the bill, but the framers of the Act did introduce what amounts to a "levy" on the capital of some foundations by establishing what the law calls a "minimum investment return" to serve as a standard for a foundation's payout to charity. The "minimum investment return" will be a percentage of the fair value of the foundation's assets. The rate is to be fixed from time to time by the Treasury in accordance with prevailing money rates and investment yields; the rate first was fixed at 6 percent. A foundation's securities must be valued at prevailing market levels, and assets that have no ready market are to be valued under regulations established by the Treasury. Each year every foundation will be required to pay out to charity either the total of its investment income and short-term capital gains (that total reduced by certain allowable deductions such as the new 4 percent tax) or the computed "minimum investment return," whichever is larger. It is in those cases where the computed minimum investment return exceeds the adjusted income of the foundation, that the foundation will eventually have to pay out of the capital an amount equal to the difference between the computed minimum investment return and the amount of the foundation's adjusted income. The aim, of course, is to force a payout on those foundations that have hitherto reported no income or little income. Failure to comply with the requirement is punishable not merely by the traditional penalty of eventual loss of exemption but by various penalty taxes, at staggered rates—characteristic of sanctions in this new legislation—which may be imposed on the foundation.[19]

Having established the concept of the payout, Congress then characteristically softened the payout provision by a "special rule," which says, in effect, that for existing foundations, that is, those in existence on May 26, 1969, the payout requirement will go into effect gradually, the minimum to be 4½ percent in 1972, 5 percent in 1973, 5½ percent in 1974, and the full 6 percent in 1975 and thereafter with no minimum requirement at all before 1972. Early in 1972, moreover, the House Ways and Means Committee recommended that the minimum payout requirement be reduced from 6 percent to 5 percent for years after 1971 and further recommended that foundations organized before May 27, 1969 be required to pay out no more than 3½ percent of their income in 1972 and 1973, 4 percent in 1974-1975, and 4½ percent in 1976-1977. Thus, for existing foundations, the full 5 percent requirement would not be applicable until 1978.[19a]

A third issue I shall consider in this chapter is that of program-related investments. These are investments in which financial return is a secondary consideration and social betterment or some purpose that coincides with the foundation's philanthropic program are primary. The Tax Reform Act specifically exempts such investments from penalties that may be imposed for an investment that would imperil a foundation's tax exemption under the Act's new regulations.[20]

Program-related investments have numerous precedents. In the past foundations have lent money to students at low rates of interest, or made "soft" loans to assist socially underprivileged groups, or invested in low-income housing and provided the tenants with what amounted to a subsidy.[21] Recently these kinds of investments have become popular again because they offer a means of providing loans or equity investments in ghetto areas where the chief beneficiaries would be members of deprived minority groups, especially Negroes. Foundations have been urged to set aside a modest portion of their capital—for example, 5 percent—for such investment or to combine with other foundations to form and endow a separate corporation the sole business of which would be that of providing "soft-loan" or social-venture capital.[22]

The proponents of this kind of foundation investment point out that, by providing resources to establish or expand high-risk enterprises in the ghettos of our cities, foundations would be complementing the grants they have made to train the poor, the unemployable, and minority victims of social and economic discrimination. By making it possible for them to establish a business or invest in one, the foundations would provide an opportunity to use the training which had been given to them and to demonstrate its value. Defenders of the policy also remind foundations that, by providing "soft-loans" or investments of this sort, they are being true to their tradition of risk-taking. Further it is urged that, among all the nonprofit organizations, the grant-making foundation is peculiarly able to make high-risk investments and suffer possible loss because it normally has only limited overhead and relatively few staff people for whose future it is responsible.

Dr. Donald Young has pointed out that the record of this type of investment is not good.[23] That fact is likely to cause those who normally make the decisions on foundation investments to view the policy with disfavor. Custodians of foundation portfolios are mindful that the law holds them accountable for making "sound" and prudent decisions, and they are perhaps understandably orthodox about investment policies. The probability is, too, that most of them would tend to shy away from any investment proposal that would use tax-exempt funds, or subsidized loans, to establish a business that, in principle at least, would compete with business that has no such advantage. Especially would this be so given the climate produced by some of Representative Patman's investigations and his concern for competitive small business. Nor is the cause of program-oriented investment likely to be aided by the fact that normally the foundation program staff is separated from those in charge of finance and investment. Nonetheless, the revival of such an investment concept is particularly timely and deserves sympathetic consideration. Private foundations ought to be casting about and experimenting with every idea that might maximize the socio-philanthropic thrust of their relatively meager resources.

Let us now turn to the fourth and final issue to be discussed in this chapter, that of the taxation of foundations. Earlier I mentioned that the federal and state governments exempt foundations from taxation in order that the government may reduce the tax burden it would have to impose were it to carry out every needed social program. As I have already noted, this policy of exempting philanthropy from taxation is being eroded, first, because many people are unaware of the rationale for exemption, or are unsympathetic toward it. Another reason is that foundations have sometimes abused the exemption privilege, especially in recent years. A third and probably the principal reason for the erosion is increasing pressure on government for new sources of revenue. Hence, most foundation directors should not have been surprised when members of the Ways and Means Committee, in mid-1969, began to talk seriously of levying a tax on foundations. Nor should they have been surprised when the advocates of a foundation tax won out and required that each foundation pay an annual excise tax of four percent on its net investment income. This is interpreted as embracing all earnings from investments—dividends, interest, rents and royalties—plus net realized capital gains, less the expense of producing the income.[24] Assuming that foundations expend about 1.5 billion dollars a year, and assuming, further, that this expenditure consists chiefly of investment income, the new tax could yield the government as much as 50 to 60 million dollars annually. The Internal Revenue Service reported actual collections from the tax totalled 24.6 million dollars in the April-June quarter of 1971 and 2.1 million dollars in the July-September quarter.

Most foundation officials are of the opinion that foundations can continue to operate satisfactorily despite the new burden. Indeed, there are those who feel that foundations might be able to assimilate successfully the entire burden of the regular corporate income tax. This may be so, although there are relatively few foundations that would care to try such a regimen. In any case, the precedent of this 4 percent excise levy makes the prospect of the normal corporate income tax being imposed upon foundations anything but academic. Nor is it a great jump from levying direct taxes on foundations to a policy of not allowing a foundation contributor to deduct his donation under estate, inheritance, and gift laws. Even the most confirmed optimist would not deny that, if this happened, foundation endowments would be threatened and, hence, the continued existence of foundations or the creation of new ones.

It is, therefore, scarcely an exaggeration to consider the 1969 breach in the foundations' tax-exemption wall as one of the most serious threats to their future that foundations have experienced. To combat that threat, foundations will be well advised to make more-sustained and better-conceived efforts than heretofore in extending public understanding of their financial relations with the government, namely, that when used honestly, tax exemptions do make it possible for foundations to exist and contribute to areas the government would otherwise be forced to sponsor and thereby appreciably reduce the tax burden. Of only slightly less importance is a second consideration, namely, that foundations do a better job than they have in informing the public about a foundation's finances. In the public reports which foundations issue, the financial section, if it exists at all, is usually the most defective. Often not even ordinary auditor's documents, such as balance sheets and income and expense statements, are provided. Virtually no report discusses the criteria which dictate the various types of investment, or identify the guidelines which govern investment policy. Rarely does a report list the corporations in which the foundation is a shareholder. When a list of corporate names is provided, there is a tendency to provide little specific information as to the number of shares held in each corporation, the value at which they are carried on the books of the foundation, and the market value of the investment. Reports are likewise deficient in the manner in which they provide information about debt securities, real estate, royalties, or other property which the foundation may own. Perhaps the government's new reporting requirements will help foundations to overcome these deficiencies if they lack the will to overcome them voluntarily.

A third part of any prescription to gain a greater degree of public understanding and tolerance of the foundations' financial operations would be that foundation directors, especially of the larger ones, recognize that they have certain economic obligations as residents to the community in which they conduct their oft far-flung operations. There is little excuse—the "man in the street" probably sees none at all—for foundations to seek to exempt themselves from real estate, sales, and other local taxes and expect other local residents to defray the cost of the municipal services which foundations enjoy. Many foundations rent quarters and they thus automatically pay for some of the services. But other foundations buy valuable property and thereby remove it from the municipal tax rolls. On the purchased sites, they occupy, tax free, what may be quite palatial quarters. Foundations could well afford to make, in lieu of local taxes, a direct contribution to the cost of municipal services. The Twentieth Century Fund has done something along this line in New York. It is a policy which the entire foundation community would be well advised to imitate. Meanwhile at least one state, New York, has taken action to narrow real property exemptions and to require payment for municipal services; and this may force foundations to pay their way locally.

NOTES—CHAPTER 7

1. *The Investment Policies of Foundations* (New York, 1967), pp. 2-3, 5-6, 13.
2. Pp. 16, 22.
3. P. x.
4. Balk, *The Free List, Property Without Taxes* (New York, 1971), pp. 10-12.
5. *Op. cit.,* p. 203.
6. *The Foundation Directory*, 4th Edition, p. xii.
7. P. 22.
8. P. viii.
9. *Op. cit.,* p. 103.
10. *Ibid.,* p. 12.
11. *Ibid.,* p. 50.
12. Ford Foundation *Annual Report* (1968), p. 74.
13. Alfred P. Sloan Foundation, *Report for 1968*, pp. 54-55.
14. See tabulation of that foundation's equities in oil and related companies in *Patman Committee Report*, 6th Installment, March 26, 1968, pp. 34-35.
15. The pertinent section of the Act is 101 (b); of the Code, 4943.
16. See generally comment by the head of the Peterson Commission on Private Philanthropy before the Senate Finance Committee reprinted in booklet entitled *Testimony to be Received, Oct. 22, 1969*, 91st Cong., 1st Sess., Washington: Government Printing Office, 1969, pp. 80 *ff*.
17. *Op. cit.,* p. 103.
18. Internal Revenue Code of 1954, Section 504 (a).
19. Tax Reform Act, Section 101 (b); Code, Section 4942.
19a. See Report on H.R. 11197. H. Rep. 92-791, 92nd Cong., 2nd Sess.

20. Act, Section 101 (b); Code, Section 4944.
21. Young and Moore, *op. cit.*, pp. 122-123; Nelson, *op. cit.*, p. 89.
22. See presentation of John G. Simon, President of Taconic Foundation, on pp. 107 *ff.* of *Proceedings*, 19th Annual Conference of the Council on Foundations, Inc., Kansas City, Mo., 1968.
23. Young and Moore, *op. cit.*, p. 123.
24. Act, Section 101 (b); Code, Section 4940.

Chapter 8

AMERICAN FOUNDATIONS ABROAD

OVER THE YEARS American foundations, especially a few wealthy, general-purpose foundations, have made grants outside the United States. In doing so, the foundations have often had to create a special corps of field representatives and other specialists to manage the enterprises or to counsel them. The unique problems these people encountered probably encouraged the foundations to become more active in identifying opportunities for using their philanthropy and in designing, initiating, and administering projects. This more intimate managerial involvement of the foundation in projects outside the United States has undoubtedly served as a precedent, and possibly a model, for increasing involvement in projects in the United States, especially during the past decade.

The major pioneer in foundation philanthropy outside the United States was the Rockefeller Foundation and institutions affiliated with it or offshoots of the Rockefeller family's philanthropies. Through a subsidiary of the Rockefeller Foundation, known as the International Health Board, efforts were made to raise standards of public health and combat endemic disease outside the United States (at the same time similar programs were carried out within the country). Through another subsidiary, now autonomous, the China Medical Board of New York, the foundation spent some 45 million dollars on the Peking Union Medical College and gave assistance to other medical and para-medical training centers outside the United States. It has been estimated that, by 1969, the Rockefeller Foundation had spent more than 150 million dollars abroad, fully a third of its entire outgo up to that time.

The global philanthropic concern of the Rockefeller Foundation was continued in the fifties and sixties to improve agricultural technology in Mexico and other Latin American states and in areas of the Far East, to improve educational facilities in Africa and elsewhere, and to combat over-population. These efforts have been supplemented by the activities of "spin-off" organizations of the Rockefeller family's philanthropic interests such as the Rockefeller Brothers Fund, the Council on Economic and Cultural Affairs, the American International Association for Economic and Social Development, and the JDR 3rd Fund.

Other American foundations support philanthropic projects abroad. Indeed the philanthropies of Andrew Carnegie in Britain and elsewhere actually antedated the Rockefeller grants outside the United States. He created the Carnegie Corporation with a special fund for certain British Commonwealth countries in 1911. The W. K. Kellogg Foundation supports medical and educational activities in Latin America. Still other American foundations of some magnitude which have occasionally made grants abroad include the Lilly Endowment and the Bollingen, Andrew Mellon, R. K. Mellon, Charles S. Mott, and Alfred P. Sloan foundations.

There are also a number of relatively small foundations which carry on modest programs outside the United States. Among them are the American-Scandinavian Foundation; the Belgian American Educational Foundation, founded by contributions made to the Hoover Commission for the Relief of Belgium after World War I; the Good Samaritan Foundation of Wilmington, Delaware, which has a small health program in Spain; and the Littauer Foundation with programs in the Near East. Still other foundations spend money to further education in international affairs. Most of the funds go to United States students and scholars but some of them may also be spent abroad. Probably the most distinguished of this type of "international" foundation is the Carnegie Endowment for International Peace, now over sixty years old, which spends much of its income in the United States to improve international law and organization and public understanding of international issues. It also maintains an office in Geneva and occasionally expends funds for projects related to its aims outside the United States.[1]

Around 1950, those in charge of the vast fortune committed to the Ford Foundation began to experiment with programs outside the United States, and in a few years initiated funding for such programs which reached levels that were three, and possibly four, times the total annual outlay abroad of all other foundations. A commentator has estimated that in recent years the average annual Ford outlay abroad has been in the neighborhood of 65 million dollars; that of the Rockefeller Foundation about 10 million dollars; and of the Carnegie Corporation, 1 million dollars.[2] If supplemented by all other American foundation payments abroad, it is estimated they account for more than 7 percent of all American foundation philanthropy.

Occasionally the average citizen has difficulty in understanding why private American foundations have been so generous abroad. Indeed even people from outside the United States, who may profit from this American generosity, are sometimes mystified by it. I remember several members of a management seminar for British students conceded that American foundation spending abroad was splendidly generous, but they could not understand how Americans justified it, especially when there were so many domestic needs.

Various explanations are offered. Some suggest that the phenomenon is a function of American industrialization and of the high level of national income and wealth. With by far the largest per capita income in the world, the United States—so it is argued—can afford to be generous towards other peoples low in the income scale. American commercial and industrial expansion overseas since World War II also obliges redirection of some of the money to its source. Indirectly, if not directly, foundations have profited materially from this expansion and therefore they too have a moral responsibility to assist with the economic and social development, especially of those nonindustrialized countries from which we take oil and other raw materials for American industry. There are even some who argue that, in many underdeveloped areas, foundation philanthropy is not merely morally desirable, but good business, neither recipients nor donors making much distinction between a foundation and a profit-making enterprise which happen to have a common family ancestry.

There are also those who suggest that at least part of the explanation of foundation generosity abroad lies in the ethnic origins of the American population and the concern of the descendants of immigrants, wealthy enough to create a foundation, for the land of their forefathers. Others find an explanation in the influence of organized religion which, historically, besides proselytizing through missions abroad, established schools, colleges, hospitals, and medical centers, creating such institutions as Robert College in Turkey, the American University of Beirut, and similar enterprises in the Near East. A generation ago, some foundation founders were not immune to this kind of mission activity and would direct that some of the largess of their newly created foundations be used to supplement and extend what the foreign missions of their respective church denominations had done. Finally there are those, usually with a Marxist ideological orientation, who suggest, rather cynically, that the entire phenomenon is simply a form of American cultural and economic imperialism.

Most of the great American foundations made it clear, at the time they were created, that their concern was worldwide. A classic statement of that concern appears in what the lawyers call the "purpose clause" of the charter of The Rockefeller Foundation that the foundation was created to "promote the well-being of mankind throughout the world." A similar clause in the Ford Foundation's formal mandate declares its purpose to be "the advancement of human welfare." There are indeed few foundations that fail to emphasize that their beneficence is not limited to America.

In the decade following World War II, the need for private foundation assistance abroad was greatly expanded when many new nations were coming into being. Fortuitously, the huge Ford Foundation was set up at this time, and its trustees declared their interest in entering the foreign field. Contributions to the development of the under-developed world by the larger American foundations raised the foreign expenditures of American foundations in the sixties to the levels mentioned earlier.

It was also these needs of the developing nations, and the efforts of the foundations to respond, that led to those departures from precedent in matters of staffing and in operations, mentioned earlier. When a private foundation spent funds abroad in the first half of the twentieth century, its *modus operandi* and limited objectives were not unlike those observed in the United States. That is, the foundation normally made grants to individuals and institutions to assist in their development or maintenance. Usually little consideration was given to the impact of such grants upon the complex of values and institutions of the society in which the recipients of the grants existed. During the fifties and sixties, however, foundations developed programs to raise a whole society's technological and administrative expertise and to create institutions for that purpose.[3] This required a sustained effort over a longer period than was traditional in foundation practice. It also required the direct involvement of foundation staff and consultants in the field and a degree of supervision of program activity by foundation personnel which, up to that time, had been the exception in domestic commitments. The managerial requirements of these foreign programs thus tended to produce a hybrid type of foundation—one that was neither a purely grant-making institution nor a purely operating foundation but something in between. About the only model for such a hybrid had been provided by the Rockefeller Foundation in carrying out its public health and agricultural development projects mentioned earlier.

In undertaking this role abroad the major difficulty the foundations faced was the relative lack of funds. Budgets for modernization can quickly become astronomical in size. Even the entire income of the three-billion dollar Ford Foundation would hardly satisfy more than a small part of the money needed to develop a country like India or Pakistan. Hence those foundations that became involved saw that they would have to fit their projects and expenditures into an overall plan for the development of a country and hope for the rest of the funds from government or international agencies. They therefore decided to apply their energies and resources to the improvement of agricultural and industrial technology. They concentrated on training the administrators and managers by establishing or improving training institutions, and by importing teachers from the more developed countries. For major institutional expenditures and maintenance of the broad developmental programs, they relied—admittedly with their trust often misplaced and their hopes frequently disappointed—upon the resources of the government of the state being aided, and upon funds from the United States government, United Nations agencies, and other states or groups of states that have accepted some responsibility for aiding developing areas.

Thus in describing its overseas development program in recent years, the Ford Foundation says that it has emphasized "training" rather than "bricks and mortar." Its specific aim has been to help "create or strengthen agencies and institutions that can provide the skills needed in agriculture, family planning, university and public-school education, science and technology, development planning, and related fields." [4] The foundation's spokesman goes on to say that "the bulk of its [the foundation's] assistance overseas is for consultants, mainly from American universities, who help establish new institutions." To carry out this responsibility, the foundation's administrative involvement has also grown apace. The three overseas offices which the foundation had established in Beirut, New Delhi, and Karachi in the early fifties had, by 1967, been increased to twenty, in Africa and the Near and Far East. They were set up "to keep in close touch with the people and institutions of the regions in which [the foundation] operates." [5]

More conventional grants, of the supportive type, have not been ignored because the directors have concentrated on development. Leading foundations, active overseas, have continued to aid colleges and universities. They have continued to make grants to promote the arts and communication; to improve scholarly exchanges between the Communist and non-Communist worlds; and to finance conferences and research projects relating to such topics as international education, the world monetary system, European economic and political integration, and population control. But even these grants have not been entirely divorced from the prevailing ideal of assisting the developing world. Thus a Ford grant to the

Centre for Educational Television Overseas, with headquarters in London, was primarily designed to assist the Centre to train personnel from developing countries. Likewise a grant to the Niels Bohr Institute in Copenhagen was designed to finance fellowships for students from developing countries. Even grants made to many American universities to train American students in the less-familiar foreign languages were chiefly intended to train personnel as consultants for developing countries.

This rather intimate and extensive involvement of America's leading foundations abroad has generally evoked praise, usually from governmental officials with experience in developing areas who are aware of the important part the foundations have in a comprehensive program of change to which their own government may also be contributing. The private foundation has frequently been able to carry out successfully many activities which the United States government, or even an international agency, would have been unable to undertake either because of local political sensitivities or because of the objections of voters and administrators in the United States or other countries. There is little question, for example, that in the case of so sensitive a subject as population control, the private American foundation has been able to make more headway abroad, initially at least, than the American government could. Management training programs, particularly programs to upgrade administrators in a developing African state, where political sensibilities and susceptibilities are concerned, are wholly appropriate for a private American foundation but less appropriate for funding by the government to which that foundation owes allegiance. Foundations can successfully sponsor and fund conferences of scientists and other intellectuals because they often can establish communications between scholars from states that are formally divided by conflicting ideologies. For example, American foundations partly funded the so-called "Pugwash" conferences during the past decade, and their support of fellowships for intellectuals from Eastern

Europe who came to the United States for study were major contributing factors to the thawing of the "Cold War" and the inauguration of the policy of "coexistence" between the Communist East and the West.

In being active outside the United States, foundations make other contributions. Usually they can mobilize staff and consultants for service abroad more easily than the government can. Because they are relatively independent of changing political tides either at home or abroad, their staffs remain *persona grata* and continue operations even when relations between governments become strained. Thus following the Arab-Israeli War of 1967, President Nasser demanded the withdrawal from Egypt of all American diplomatic representatives. The Ford Foundation staff was allowed to remain throughout and was able to continue with projects that otherwise would have been stopped.

In evaluating the performance of the foundation which has been most active abroad, that is, the Ford Foundation, Dr. Walter E. Ashley stated that "there have been a few spectacular successes and some complete failures; most projects occupy the gray area in between. Any evaluation of what they have accomplished must be to some degree subjective." [6] He goes on to say that Ford money might have yielded more impressive results if the directors had concentrated on a few states—perhaps on as few as two states. He also suggests that a larger percentage of the funds ventured might have been spent for agricultural research and demonstration projects with the aim of increasing agricultural yields and living standards —essentially what the Rockefeller Foundation has been specializing in over the years. As an illustration he points to the International Rice Research Institute in the Philippines, a jointly sponsored Ford-Rockefeller project, which he describes as one of the "greatest successes of American philanthropy overseas." A somewhat similar project, and perhaps equally valuable, is the recently established center for African tropical agriculture at Ibadan.

At the same time, Dr. Ashley is by no means absolutely certain that concentration always is the wiser course. The leaders of developing nations know that foundations can respond more promptly and more flexibly than other possible sources of money. They are aware of the foundation's interest in "institution building" and basic social reform, and of the foundation's ability to engage in such activity on a nonpolitical basis. They also approach a foundation because of their desire to supplement public funds from abroad and thus avoid too great reliance on government-to-government aid programs, or because of "dissatisfaction with other agencies." In any case, concludes Dr. Ashley, the issue of dispersal versus concentration in foundation foreign aid "should be left open, but should be the subject of constant appraisal in the light of new developments." [7]

Surprisingly little criticism has been offered to dampen the praise directed at contemporary foundation activity abroad. To be sure, an occasional editorial writer or industrialist, or possibly some politician, may grumble about "shortchanging America." He may add that the money doled out on behalf of a foreign country has probably been wasted. The critic may suggest that the real motive in spending foundation money for projects outside the United States is to provide tax-free fulfillment of a foundation staff man's well-known desire to travel around the world. For the greater part these are unwarranted, if not meaningless, criticisms. Where warranted, they are usually negligible. Slightly more serious criticism was voiced some years ago by the Patman Committee when its head took exception to foundation largess abroad because it had the alleged effect of aggravating the apparently chronic deficit in America's international account.

Those who look askance at foreign aid by foundations are not likely to constitute the major obstacle in the future. Rather the chief obstacle may well be the difficulty of maintaining the foundations' reputation for objectivity and political independence, and especially their freedom from influence by their own government. As I have already noted, it is these attributes or, at any rate, the reputation of possessing them, that have made the American foundation a corporate *persona grata* abroad and have made possible so many special services on its part that other organizations, including its own government, could not have rendered.

It was these attributes that were seriously compromised some years ago when the Central Intelligence Agency used a number of private foundations—some said as many as fifty— as conduits for public money to be spent on CIA projects abroad. One or two of the foundations affected had major reputations as philanthropic agencies, although others seemed to have been created, or revived for the purpose. The names of the individuals involved also included a few influential figures in major American foundations.[8] These foundations may have been inspired by patriotic motives, but their cooperation made it all too apparent that there is validity to the charges of critics, especially of chronically hostile foreign critics, that the American foundation, operating abroad, is really an instrument of the United States Government. For the long run, the CIA-foundation episode may have done the foundations a good turn. It provides an unambiguous illustration of how quickly and how thoroughly a foundation's capacity to render its unique service abroad can be jeopardized and its reputation as a private philanthropic organization compromised if it fails to take seriously the need to remain outside the orbit of direct government influence and nourish its independence. As a result, in the future, both foundation administrators and government agencies may well seek to remain disassociated. It is a condition that all friends of the private foundation hope will not be challenged again.

The independence of the private foundation abroad also could be strengthened if it would take up a greater number of cooperative projects. In this way some of the small foundations could participate in projects that otherwise would be too expensive for them and make service more attractive to their personnel. At the same time such cooperation could reduce somewhat the hegemony of America's largest private foundation.

Cooperative efforts by private American foundations could be extended and insurance against overt governmental interference strengthened and confirmed, if the aid of some of the newer foundations, established elsewhere in the world, could be enlisted.[9] The new *Directory of European Foundations*, published by Russell Sage Foundation in 1969, lists a surprising number of Western European foundations, most of them relatively new. The majority have developed little of the expertise of large American foundations, especially when it comes to operating outside national boundaries. A team approach to foreign problems, in collaboration with experienced American foundations, could provide these newer Western European and other foundations with a valuable and not too costly introduction to a broader and less parochial responsibility and help insure to them and their American counterparts the reputation for independence from their respective governments and an operational means of guaranteeing such independence. Some years ago, John J. McCloy, then Chairman of the Board of the Ford Foundation, developed this theme of collaboration with Western European foundations.[10] The wisdom of his endorsement at that time has been confirmed by some of the events we have just chronicled and by the expanding opportunity for private foundation philanthropy beyond the confines of the industrialized West.

NOTES—CHAPTER 8

1. See "Fifty Years in the Service of Peace with Justice," undated pamphlet published by the Endowment, New York.
2. For these estimates, much other factual material, and some of my editorializing, I am indebted to an as yet unpublished

work entitled *Philanthropy and Government: A Study of Ford Foundation's Overseas Activity*, by a former student of mine, Dr. Walter E. Ashley.

3. Harvey P. Hall, "An American Foundation and Technical Assistance," Ford Foundation Publication, undated, p. 5.
4. Ford Foundation, *Annual Report* (1967), p. 46.
5. *Ibid.*, p. 46.
6. *Op. cit.*, p. 173.
7. *Ibid.*, pp. 174-175.
8. See an excellent resumé by Richard Harwood in the files of the *Washington Post* (February 26, 1967), Section E.
9. See also Smith, "Philanthropy in Asia," *Foundation News* (July-August, 1969), p. 133, and Stromberg, *Philanthropic Foundations in Latin America* (Russell Sage Foundation, New York, 1969).
10. Ace International Seminar for Diplomats at Schloss Klessheim, Salzburg, Austria, August 16, 1965.

Chapter 9

COMPANY-SPONSORED FOUNDATIONS

FOR THE RELATIVELY unsophisticated it is perhaps startling to encounter the names of many outstanding American business and industrial enterprises in the names of foundations. Thus the petroleum industry supports such foundations as the Gulf Oil Fund, the American Oil Foundation, the Pan American Petroleum Foundation, the Esso Education Foundation, the Shell Companies Foundation, and the Standard Oil Foundation (of Indiana). The tire industry has the B. F. Goodrich Foundation, the Firestone Foundation, and the General Tire Foundation, among others. Automotive manufacturers are represented by the White Charitable Trust and the Ford Motor Company Fund. Lumber, steel, glass, and aluminum can list such charitable industries as United States Steel, Alcoa, National Steel, Libby-Owens-Ford, Corning Glass, Inland Steel-Ryerson, Armco, and Weyerhauser. There is a Briggs and Stratton Corporation Foundation as well as General Electric and Westinghouse Electric foundations. There are also foundations for Bell and Howell, Crown-Zellerbach, Borg-Warner, Caterpillar, International Harvester, John Deere, Procter and Gamble, Cutler-Hammer, Boeing, Allis Chalmers, and International Paper Company.

Food and allied industries contribute to the foundation directory such names as Oscar Mayer, Swift, H. J. Heinz, Carnation, Borden, General Foods, and Gerber Baby Foods, not to ignore Schlitz and Anheuser-Busch. Merchandising contributes such philanthropic names as Marshall Field, Sears Roebuck, Altman, and May Company Stores, among others. Banks, too, support foundations, including Chase Manhattan Bank, Chemical Bank New York Trust, Morgan Guaranty Trust, Bank of America-Giannini, and Manufacturers Hanover Trust. Even auditing firms like Haskins and Sells have a foundation and so, too, does the stock exchange firm of Merrill, Lynch, Pierce, Fenner and Smith. Indeed, there is scarcely a major corporate entity in the United States that has not found it advisable to establish a charitable "foundation," "trust," or "fund."

For the lack of public awareness of the corporate invasion of the foundation field there is more than a little justification. As we shall see later, few company-sponsored foundations had been created prior to World War II, most having been created with America's entry into that conflict and especially during the Korean imbroglio between 1950 and 1954. Because the company-based foundation is a quite recent phenomenon, the general public has had little opportunity to become acquainted with it. Indeed descriptions of its operation and of the scope and quality of its philanthropy have only just begun to attract the serious attention of analysts and researchers of the foundations.[1]

Legally, a company-sponsored foundation is similar to one begun by families. The company-sponsored foundation may be set up as a corporation or a trust, and, therefore, there is technically no difference between the Ford Foundation and the Ford Motor Company Fund. The only real difference exists in the fact that the first happens to have been created by the Ford family and the second, by the corporate entity known as the Ford Motor Company. The formal purpose of a company-sponsored foundation, moreover, is to engage in philanthropy, and it accordingly enjoys the same degree of tax exemption as a family foundation. Nevertheless, the purposes and behavior of a company-sponsored foundation differ somewhat from the family-originated foundation and hence warrant special treatment.

Industry and allied profit-making enterprises have traditionally been a source of contributions to charitable enterprises. Especially has this been true in communities in which corporate administrative headquarters or divisional offices or plants are located. As anyone in charge of a United Fund drive is aware, company gifts are made rather regularly to community chests, hospitals, and other eleemosynary causes, the rationale being that the company thus aids its employees, who are residents of the community, and proves that it is a responsible community "citizen." Prior to 1936, such company contributions could be deducted as a business expense provided they could be described as such. Since that year, however, the federal government has allowed a business enterprise to donate and deduct as much as 5 percent from taxable income for charitable purposes, and the enterprise can make these donations to virtually any tax-exempt, nonprofit organization (including a company-created foundation if there is one) and to public bodies. These donations no longer have to qualify as "business expenses."

Traditionally, corporate largess was distributed directly

without an intermediate agency such as a foundation and most corporate largess is still so distributed. The more generous policy which the framers of the nation's tax system offered corporate philanthropy after 1936 suggested, at least to some corporate officials, that there were administrative and possibly other advantages to establishing a company-organized and company-controlled, although nominally independent, foundation.*

Nevertheless, creation of such foundations lagged. In a tabulation prepared in 1964 by Emerson Andrews for The Foundation Center, it was revealed that only twenty company-sponsored foundations had been created before 1938 and that prior to 1950 a total of 487 had been set up. By 1950, however, the idea had begun to take hold, and between 1950 and 1953, 698 had been created. From 1954 to 1957, 264 additional company foundations came into being.[2] By the time The Foundation Center published its third *Directory* in 1967, it listed 1472 company-sponsored foundations that met the requirements for inclusion. These were said to control about 6 percent of all assets held by foundations and to be responsible for about 15 percent of all foundation grants and expenditures.[3]

Two developments were at least partially responsible for the sudden increase in the number of business-sponsored foundations in the 1950s. The first was the initiative taken by certain active or retired heads of some of the nation's larger corporations to persuade their colleagues to move business giving up to new levels of generosity and sophistication. Corporate leaders such as Frank W. Abrams of Standard Oil of New Jersey, Alfred P. Sloan, Jr. of General Motors, Irving Olds of United States Steel, Walter Paepcke of the Container Corporation, and a number of others argued that business should take advantage of the government's new liberality concerning corporate donations and that, in addition to discharging its traditional community responsibility, a major company

---

* For some of these alleged advantages, see pp. 124-125.

should make gifts on a national level which provided no direct and immediate advantage even as respects its public relations. Instead, they said, gifts should have a long-range objective of benefitting society, the company deriving only an indirect advantage.

These leaders were especially interested in aiding higher education and scientific research in the universities. They argued that the colleges and universities were the sources of trained manpower for industry and business generally, and provided the laboratories for pure research, the results of which industry normally exploited. Hence, though gifts for general support of these institutions or of their students or faculties, or project support of basic research, offered no immediate *quid pro quo*, the institutions obviously had a moral claim on such support. Never wholly explicit, but clearly an additional motivating factor, for at least some of these corporate leaders, was their hope that generous donations from industry would eventually eliminate, or at least reduce, the dependence of private colleges and universities on tax sources for their maintenance and growth. The philanthropic policy of these leaders also received encouragement from the courts. Contemporary judicial decisions provided liberal interpretations of corporate charter clauses dealing with donations, and recognized a kind of common-law authority of corporate officers to make gifts for which there was no direct, or immediately discernible, advantage to the corporate donor.[4]

In a relatively short time, steps were taken to implement the ideas of these business leaders. They, themselves, were instrumental in creating the Council for Financial Aid to Education, intended to popularize corporate giving to higher education. Their inspiration was also apparent in the establishment of the National Fund for Medical Education, intended to procure corporate funds for medical schools and hospitals, and in the creation of more than thirty state and regional "foundations" by means of which colleges and universities could, if they so desired, collaborate in soliciting funds from individual companies, and distribute the proceeds among themselves according to a formula agreed upon in advance. Industry's own response to this challenge, by some of its senior leaders, was to create, and in a few instances endow fairly generously, a number of company foundations which—so it was said—would be at least nominally independent of the creating company. Presumably, too, these would be able to cope with the proposed new range of business philanthropy and with the more complex responsibilities which such new philanthrophy entailed.

This response to the Abrams-Sloan-Olds challenge, in the way of new company-sponsored foundations, probably would have been far less enthusiastic had it not been for a second contemporary development which encouraged such creations. This was the high excess-profits tax that was levied during the Korean War. Added to the 48 percent of the combined normal tax and surtax on income, the excess-profits tax brought the maximum tax liability of a corporation to 82 percent. Thus it actually cost a corporation only 18 cents on each dollar it contributed to its foundation. As Professor Nelson has observed, "It is possible that tax considerations have been of special importance in the decision to make large capital grants to company-sponsored foundations." [5] His own tabulations indicate that during the years the excess-profits tax was levied, the assets of some company-sponsored foundations were increased the most.[6] The assets of 169 company-based foundations, including forty of the largest, rose from 138.5 million dollars to 341.5 million dollars, an increase of some 147 percent.

Proponents of company-supported foundations now began to supply a rationale which took advantage of the contemporary tax climate and the desire of some of the business leaders for a more advanced form of business philanthropy. In years when profits were good, it was suggested, the business-based foundation could receive and hold the amount in excess of that which the company normally contributed to charity for the leaner years, when profits were not so good, thus "evening out" contributions. The excess could also be frozen as foundation endowment and gradually build up the foundation's resources to a level where it could operate independently of the founding business and make its own long-range philanthropic plans. The foundation might then—or so it was suggested—indulge in the kind of project planning and multiple-year commitments that characterize the more advanced type of private family foundation—a role which would obscure and eventually obliterate the somewhat philistine origin of the company-sponsored foundation.[7]

On the whole, this type of foundation does not appear to have contributed greatly to the volume of giving by business, especially to higher education, the objective closest to the heart of those business leaders who sought to inaugurate a new era of corporate giving in the early fifties. In 1965 it is estimated that American corporations gave 300 million dollars to education. This was 0.37 percent of net income before taxes. They gave a little more than 1 percent to all causes—which was somewhat more than a fifth of what corporations could have given under the 5 percent maximum allowed by government.[8] In the early sixties it is estimated that corporations, including their foundations, were still providing only some 14 percent of all gifts to higher education, corporate giving falling below that of other private sectors.[9]

An altogether too likely a reason for this disappointing performance is the fact that relatively few business-sponsored foundations have succeeded in building up reserves and endowments. Here and there, to be sure, a business-based foundation became reasonably well endowed either because reserves were gradually built up from the founding company's contributions or by becoming the recipient of a major capital grant from the founding company. Thus in 1966 when the Patman Committee secured information on the assets of foundations of all types, there were at least fourteen business-sponsored foundations with assets, at market, of 10 million dollars or more. One of the fourteen, Alcoa, had more than 80 million dollars. Five of the fourteen, Gulf Oil, Standard of Indiana, General Electric, Sears Roebuck, and Firestone, each held between 25 and 45 million dollars. All the others had portfolios that ranged in value from 10 million to 17 million dollars. These included such foundations as those of International Paper, United States Steel, Burlington Industries, Republic Steel, Pittsburgh Plate Glass, and Phelps-Dodge.[10] But even these fourteen continued to rely on the founding company to make up annual deficits in their respective grant programs or determined their grant programs after the parent company's end-of-the-year profits position had been ascertained by its auditors and the level of the company's contribution to the foundation had been calculated. As for the great majority of the company-sponsored foundations on Mr. Patman's list, foundation-owned assets were negligible. For their programs of giving they were almost wholly dependent upon annual appropriations by the founding company.

The degree of dependence on the sponsoring company of even the wealthier business-based foundations becomes even more apparent in Professor Nelson's analysis of the endowment income of those company-sponsored foundations which he studied. Of the 177 foundations to which he directed his attention in 1966, some had no endowment at all. Of the 42 largest in this group of 177, most of which had some endowment income, only six had incomes large enough to finance more than 60 percent of expenditures. For half of the 42, investment income accounted for "a significant though usually minor fraction of expenditure," and for the entire group of 177, investment income accounted for only 22.3 percent of total expenditure.[11] It is perhaps superfluous to add that any class of foundations that is compelled to rely for three-quarters of its expenditure on the annual budget of a founding business can hardly develop an independent and long-range program of giving.

If most company-sponsored foundations did not succeed

in becoming independent of the founding company (or did not try to do so), so too did they fail to rid themselves of the managerial structure that tied them to the sponsoring company. In most cases, the company bureaucracy continued to double for the foundation. The latter rarely commanded the services of an independent staff, whose first loyalty would be to the cause of philanthropy and who would be free to pursue a philanthropic policy divorced from the internal managerial and public-relations requirements of the parent company. Even the larger company-sponsored foundations could rarely point to more than one or two officers whose time was fully committed to the foundation. As likely as not, moreover, foundation officers were on the company payroll for at least part of their salary, and the salary they were paid was determined by the parent company's salary classification for executive personnel. Such foundation employees also continued to share in the parent company's fringe benefits, if any, and to enjoy other company perquisites. Moreover, even when program officers had been employed who devoted all their time to foundation business, the service and financial side of the foundation's operations was usually entrusted to corporate employees or to "outside experts" who served the corporation on a contractual basis.

In all this left-handed management by a business of its foundation, an especially censurable practice, at least until recently, was that of selecting, as a foundation program officer, an employee of the parent company who was close to retirement age or had already passed it. His age was quite likely to inhibit anything venturesome or imaginative in foundation policy. Moreover, as a company alumnus, his philanthropic decisions were almost certain to be geared closely to the values that he had developed as a past employee of the sponsoring company or department.

In short, the limitations imposed upon the business foundation's resources and upon its freedom of managerial action make it difficult, if not impossible, for business-sponsored foun-

dation managers to live up to the expectations of those who
had looked with favor upon the expansion of these foundations in the fifties.

Nor is it difficult to understand other managerial weaknesses of the business foundation, for example, its cavalier
attitude towards its obligation to issue an acceptable public
report or any report at all. For most of these foundations,
the reason for the failure to report regularly or for their
tendency to be cryptic and uninformative in their reports
about their grants, staff, investments, and other particulars, is
obvious. Almost any sponsoring business would be embarrassed
if it had to spell out to the public just how dependent the
foundation is on the parent company for resources, how
minuscule are most of its grants, and how limited in number
and ability its staff. The foundation or the company would be
especially embarrassed if either had to reveal how small the
intellectual and monetary dimensions of the authorized grants
really are and—for most business-sponsored foundations—how
intimately grants are correlated with the policies and interests of the founding business.

Examples of the latter are numerous. A foundation, whose
parent is an oil company, will try to find a way to improve
native managerial and technical skills in undeveloped areas
where oil is being extracted. A foundation whose parent is a
pharmaceutical house will normally favor grants to schools
and departments of pharmacology, or to medical schools generally, and to medical research. Sometimes this "strictly business" role of a company-sponsored foundation is conceded
without making excuses. In one of its recent public reports,
the Smith, Kline and French Foundation states quite candidly
that its trustees are instructed to "endeavor to give preferen-
tial consideration to charitable, educational, and scientific uses
and purposes which may be related, directly or indirectly, to
the welfare of Smith, Kline and French employees and to its
interest as a corporation." [12] In so saying, this distinguished
pharmaceutical house is being honest. What it suggests, more-

over, is perfectly legal and even socially useful. Its foundation is nonetheless a "captive" agency and an independent philanthropic course is, by definition, denied to it.

There are exceptions. The United States Steel Foundation is such an exception. So, too, are such business-based foundations as Corning Glass, Cummins Engine, Esso, General Electric, International Paper, Pittsburgh Plate Glass, Sears Roebuck, and Shell Companies.[13] Occasionally these, and other company-sponsored foundations have supported programs which, for ingenuity of design, duration of commitment, and response to broad social demand, rank with the best of the programs of the professional, general-purpose foundation. In the main, however, it must be conceded that the programs of company foundations suggest little advance beyond the philanthropic tenets of the corporate donations officer or committee.

Some critics of the company-sponsored foundation hold that an attempt to mix business and professional philanthropy is a mistake. They contend that the only legitimate philanthropy for a business is traditional "business philanthropy," that is, donations for which there is an immediate *quid pro quo* in the form of good will in a community or improved employee morale or efficiency. Such philanthropy can even be justified as a business expense. Philanthropy of the kind in which a mature, family-derived foundation is likely to engage cannot, in their opinion, be so justified. That kind of philanthropy, they argue, adds unnecessarily to the cost and hence, usually, to the price of the company's service or commodity. It may thus penalize the customer and weaken the company's own competitive position. Critics also look askance at a business-sponsored foundation because it offers the parent company the opportunity to exploit tax benefits that are legally questionable or at least contrary to the public interest. The charge has possibly been justified in some recent cases where heavily appreciated assets have been donated by the business to its foundation for a tax credit and to allow continuing indirect control of the donated assets through the foundation. Abuses of this nature, however, do not appear to have been widespread.[14]

In summary, the company-sponsored foundation seems to be, at best, a creation with a dubious value because this type of foundation has failed to fulfill the expectations of those who looked to it to establish a new and more imaginative philanthropic role for American business, one equivalent to, or at least not far removed from, the role of the large, privately endowed, general-purpose foundation. Moreover, the credibility of all foundations has been weakened by the claims of some of the executives of business-sponsored foundations that they are independent of the sponsoring businesses and are engaged in professional philanthropy. In far too many cases such claims simply do not square with the facts.

As we move farther into the 1970s, it is possible that philanthropic and business policy will become increasingly similar, especially if industry does try to deal with some of the social imperatives such as extending employment opportunity to minority groups and stemming pollution of the environment. What, in another age, might have been regarded as business philanthropy will thus come to be regarded as a necessary part of normal industrial behavior. However, the discharge of such obligations will require decisions from those directly in command of the business. They cannot very well be delegated even to closely controlled foundations. In the long run, therefore, foundations, as vehicles for business philanthropy, may well become outmoded by the changing social obligations of industry.

Even so, right now, business and industry could do themselves a service, and aid the cause of philanthropy, if they sought to dispel some of the ambiguities surrounding their current exploitation of company-sponsored foundations. They could do so, first, by cutting loose, and placing in the "philanthropic domain," those foundations which they have created and to which they have given at least a modest endowment— in other words, by making the financially stronger and stable foundations truly independent. Second, they could review the whole institutional structure of industrial and business giving and, where possible, fold up company foundations that really are not serving a purpose and hand responsibility for business donations back to the corporate officers. Third, wherever it is decided, for any reason, to continue a closely associated company-sponsored foundation, they should permit it to serve the real but hitherto too often concealed aim of acting as a public-relations or "good-will" arm of the company. Such actions and avowals would not be likely to cause much eyebrow-lifting in the Internal Revenue Service, and they would clearly help to dissipate some of the current misunderstanding and suspicion about the company-sponsored foundation. By clarifying their proper role in the field of philanthropy, business and industry would improve their own "image" and the reputation of the whole of foundation philanthropy.

NOTES—CHAPTER 9

1. See Frank M. Andrews, *A Study of Company-Sponsored Foundations* (New York, 1962), and Nelson, *op. cit.*, pp. 128 *ff*. Russell Sage Foundation has announced the forthcoming publication on this subject by two eminent authorities, namely, Fremont-Smith, *Corporate Philanthropy*, and Nelson, *Economic Factors in the Growth of Corporate Giving*. See also the Conference Board's booklet #6 in its Studies in Public Affairs, entitled *20 Company Sponsored Foundations—Programs and Policies*.
2. *The Foundation Directory*, 2nd Edition (New York, 1964), p. 32.
3. 3rd Edition, pp. 28-32.
4. See, for example, *A. P. Smith Manufacturing Company v. Ruth F. Barlow et al.*, 13 N.J. 145 (1952), 346 U.S. 861 (1953); *Union Pacific R.R. Company v. Trustees, Inc.*, 8

Utah 101 (1958). See also the discussion of legal development of corporate charitable giving in Thomas, *Policies Underlying Corporate Giving* (Englewood Cliffs, New Jersey), 1966, pp. 16-29.

5. *The Investment Policies of Foundations*, p. 126.
6. *Idem*, pp. 126-131.
7. See, for example, Frank M. Andrews, *op. cit.*, pp. 26-27.
8. See *Special Report* of Editorial Projects for Education, Inc. (1968), a nonprofit organization associated with the American Alumni Council.
9. Levi and Vorsanger, *Patterns of Giving to Higher Education*, published by the American Council on Education (1968), p. 11.
10. See *Patman Committee Report*, Sixth Installment, March 26, 1968, pp. 228-259.
11. Nelson, *op. cit.*, p. 136. It is only fair to remind readers that Professor Nelson's data do not go beyond 1960.
12. *Annual Report* (1968), p. 24.
13. See, for example, "Corning Glass Works Foundation Special Report," *Foundation News*, Vol. IX, No. 6 (November 1968), pp. 157-161.
14. The Patman Committee has made charges of this nature; see, for example, *Patman Committee Report*, Sixth Installment, March 26, 1968, p. 18.

Chapter 10

THE COMMUNITY FOUNDATION

THE COMMUNITY FOUNDATION, or, to give it its older name, the community trust, has several characteristics which set it apart from other types of foundations. In the first place, as its name implies, it concentrates its philanthropy upon a city, or a metropolitan area, or possibly the county in which it is located. Another unique aspect of this kind of foundation is the fact that the greater part of its assets is in the form of many separate trusts. The community foundation is not normally the trustee; that responsibility is usually confided to the trust department of various banks. Thus the New York Community Trust describes itself as "a composite of almost 200 charitable funds dedicated to diverse purposes. . . ." [1] Still another unique feature is the sizable proportion of the foundation revenue that is designated for special beneficiaries or that is otherwise restricted as to purpose and beneficiary. Finally, a fourth special feature is the fact that many community foundations are not incorporated. Although today more community foundations are being incorporated, with a charter from the state, or set up as a trust in their own right, some are still the result of a mere resolution adopted by the community's banks to provide an organization through which they can distribute the revenue arising from the charitable trusts of which they are trustees.

The first of the community foundations, known as the Cleveland Foundation, was created in 1914 by Frederick H. Goff, then president of the Cleveland Trust Company. He was encouraged to start the foundation by members of his own bank's staff and by fellow banking and trust officers of the American Bankers Association. Apparently Leonard Ayres, formerly of the staff of Russell Sage Foundation, was an influential adviser. The Goff plan for a foundation has been copied and improved. Thus the trust instrument, set up by Goff, named five leading Cleveland citizens as members of a "distribution committee" which was empowered to recommend grants and choose beneficiaries in the case of all charitable trusts administered by the bank. Goff's plan was altered somewhat when the New York Community Trust was organized in 1923 by several banks to administer charitable trusts in the New York area—by 1928 as many as 18. These banks pooled their trusts by an appropriate resolution and set up a committee to represent each bank. This intermediate "trustee committee," necessitated by the multiplicity of banks, selected a minority of the members of a distribution committee; the majority of the committee was designated by community governmental, educational, and industrial leaders and heads of local bar and medical associations. This revised form of organization, which accommodated several banks, thereafter became fairly general. Later management was improved when many of the larger community foundations enlisted the services of a director and auxiliary staff, operating either full-time or part-time, to make investigations and reports to the distribution committee on community needs and possible benefactions, and otherwise to "professionalize" the foundation's philanthropy.

From the point of view of a bank or trustee, the community foundation is of considerable value. As we have noted, the foundation provides the counsel of leading citizens in disbursing that portion of trust income not designated as to beneficiary. Moreover with a foundation to back him, a banker can counsel prospective settlors of trusts against making their charitable purpose too inflexible in the face of changing cultural and technological conditions. Of course, because of the existence of a foundation the banker also hopes to attract trusts for the income from the high fees which such trusts usually provide. Indeed a somewhat too enthusiastic concern by controlling banks for the profit derived from the managed trusts continues to be a liability of many community foundations.

Like the cause of charity generally, the community foundation suffered during the depression years of the thirties, but it entered upon a period of sustained popularity after World War II.[2] In 1964, Professor Nelson identified 183 active community foundations in the United States and estimated that they accounted for about 2.5 percent of all the foundation expenditures and for about 3 percent of all the invested capital owned by foundations.[3] Investigations by The Foundation Center in 1967, limited to 100 community foundations, estimated that their expenditures in the United States were about 2 percent of all foundation expenditures and that they possessed (or advised on) about 3 percent of all the invested capital that all foundations held.[4] Of the twelve largest community foundations, the original one, the Cleveland Foundation, controlled assets valued at 100 million dollars. Three others, the New York Community Trust, the Boston Committee of the Permanent Charity Fund, and the Chicago Community Trust, each had access to assets in excess of 60 million dollars; while the assets attributed to each of the remaining eight foundations were well above the 10 million dollar mark.

In some respects, the distribution committee of the community foundation can be compared to the board of trustees of other types of foundations. The distribution committee does not manage investments, as do boards of trustees, that being confided to the banks. On the other hand, the committee, like a board, can authorize expenditures and hence control the foundation program. At any rate, the committee usually does have the authority to spend, for bona fide local philanthropic purposes, whatever income the associated bank trustees make available from the respective trusts they administer. The distribution committee is subject only to whatever specific limitations the settlor of a trust may have imposed. In a table which Mrs. Wilmer Rich, an authority on community foundations, prepared in 1961, she indicated that, of the total 1959 income of some 77 community foundations, about 46.5 percent was entirely unrestricted and its distribution was therefore wholly within the discretion of the distribution committee; 22.9 percent was intended to benefit particular causes or particular areas of philanthropy, such as education or health care; and 30.6 percent was designated, that is, intended to benefit named agencies.[5]

As might be expected, the quality of the philanthropy dispensed by each community foundation varies. In a few cases, most of the funds that come within a foundation's discretionary spending competence are likely to be used to make up operational deficits of local hospitals or welfare agencies or, possibly, of some cultural enterprise like the symphony orchestra. Or they may be used to round out the annual total budgeted for the United Fund or the local community chest. An analysis of the spending of some 55 community foundations in 1959 revealed that slightly more than half of the revenue supplemented the operations budget of community enterprises.

Apparently quite a number of community foundations also accept what, in their jargon, are known as "in-and-out gifts." These are contributions made to a foundation by an individual or corporation, usually at the end of a calendar or fiscal year, and usually for tax-purposes. The gifts are held by the foundation for distribution at some later date when the beneficiary has been decided upon. Although funds thus given to the foundation are technically removed from any further discretionary control by the donor, the foundation normally consults with him before finally disposing of the proceeds of his gift, and wherever possible, follows his wishes. Philanthropic purists sometimes criticize the community foundation for such activities, insisting that in undertaking them the foundation is being used for tax advantages and as a mere conduit for funds the purpose of which others than the foundation will define. The criticism is not without merit. However, a well-led community foundation can exercise considerable constructive influence over the primary donor in directing the proceeds of "in-and-out" gifts to the better causes. Indeed it can, and does, solicit gifts and often succeeds in persuading a donor to allow the foundation complete freedom in spending the proceeds.

Support of local, usually conventional, charitable enterprises and parcelling out funds in accordance with a donor's wishes, which are also usually conventional, will undoubtedly continue among the principal concerns of community foundations. Nevertheless, many of them are developing a more sophisticated kind of philanthropy. The representative sampling of community foundation expenditures in 1959, to which I already alluded, showed that more than 38 percent was directed towards capital purposes, that is, one-time grants for structures or basic equipment for community institutions such as libraries, schools, hospitals, and colleges. In that same sampling it was ascertained that almost 10 percent of the available funds were allocated to projects identified as "re-search" and "experiment or demonstration." These involved, among other projects, community engineering surveys of public utilities, research services for primary and secondary schools, expanding operations of the Boy Scout organization in underprivileged neighborhoods, relating the clinical work of social service agencies with the curricula of schools of social work, and providing a curriculum to assist registered nurses to qualify as public-health nurses.[6]

Similarly, in a recent article, the director of the Hartford Foundation for Public Giving, a community foundation, stated that his foundation does not contribute to the annual fund-raising campaigns of the local community chest but that it often makes a grant to chest agencies for "surveys, demon-stration projects, equipment, and sometimes new buildings." He adds that within a recent twelve-month period, the founda-tion had funded "innovative programs in such diverse areas as drug addiction, alcoholism, planned parenthood, disillu-sioned youth, and education for the disadvantaged. . . ."[7]

Substantively too, the broad areas in which community foundations make most of their grants are not much different from those in which foundations in general are active. The three principal areas are social welfare, which embraces almost half of all grants, and health and education, which together account for about 44 percent of expenditures. The Greater Cincinnati Foundation, for example, indicated recently that 62 percent had been devoted to one-time capital expenditures, 23 percent to the solution of community problems, or their prevention, and only 15 percent to help meet agency operating deficits. As to broad substantive areas, 58 percent of this foundation's expenditures were allocated to the field of health and welfare, 36 percent to education, and 6 percent for gen-eral cultural purposes.[8]

Opportunities for the community foundation to indulge in more creative giving will probably increase as the value of its services becomes better known. Effective counseling of prospective donors will eventually pay off in wiser philanthropy, including more contributions to the foundation which can determine the beneficiary and the conditions affecting the actual use of the funds. By incorporating itself and becoming a legal entity, the community foundation may acquire greater influence in determining the purposes of a new trust or in keeping the trust discretionary even though the funds are still placed with an associated bank as trustee. It may also succeed in reducing bank charges and correspondingly increasing the outgo to charity. Here and there, moreover, a community foundation and a local family foundation have cooperated in donating funds for some project. The community foundation may make the initial grant to establish a local social-welfare or cultural project and the family foundation then assumes the continuing financial obligation.

The performance of the community foundation has been enhanced by the creation in Chicago in 1949 by Frank D. Loomis of a National Committee on Foundations and Trusts for Community Welfare. In 1957 this became the National Council on Community Foundations which, in 1964, changed its name to the Council on Foundations. Led during its formative years by Mrs. Wilmer Rich, and directed since her retirement by David Freeman, this organization has done for the community foundation and affiliated organizations what needs doing for the foundation community in general. It has stimulated constructive cooperation among its constituent foundations and established counseling and information services for them which have been especially useful to the less well staffed organization. The Council has also provided the community foundations with a spokesman and a representative before the public and has sought to inculcate in its membership respect for high standards of administrative performance and fiscal integrity.

The Council conducts an annual conference on foundation matters in one of the nation's major cities. The conference agenda include the more important current issues affecting philanthropy and provide an opportunity for a constructive dialogue between the Council's foundation constituency and outstanding philanthropists and philanthropic experts.[9] To even the most casual observer, it is clear that the Council's performance has been a unique one, that it has been a constructive performance, and that its service has been reflected in the improved service of the community foundation.

The community foundation is sometimes considered to be the Cinderella among foundations. The staff of the more affluent general-purpose and intermediate family foundations are inclined to regard it as such, and even its own spokesmen often assume an apologetic stance when discussing its achievements and shortcomings. Whatever its limitations, however, and despite its somewhat conventional philanthropic role, there is much about the community foundation's history that is praiseworthy; and its organization and administrative experience offer lessons that could benefit its sister institutions among the family-derived foundations, not excluding the largest.

One of those lessons is the value of cooperation among foundations in pooling experience and opinions about projects, grantees, and philanthropic needs to the end of securing maximum value for the philanthropic dollar. Another, closely related to this first lesson, is the implication of the occasional use of the community foundation as the "remainder man" of a family foundation following the death of the donor. The community foundation thereby provides a cooperative and professional means of maintaining a philanthropy and discourages the continued existence of foundations too small to justify their administrative cost. Still another lesson is inherent in the community foundation's form of government, particularly in its insistence upon securing a wide sampling of professional, vocational, and cultural interests on its governing body. A fourth lesson is that implicit in the effort which the community foundation has made to keep philanthropy up to date and to avoid or remove the influence of mortmain.

Finally in this catalogue to which other items might be added, mention should be made of the community foundation's pioneering a central service agency, namely, the Council on Foundations, which I have described. As foundations in general move towards creation of a body to advise them, provide a continuous dialogue among them on matters of common interest, represent them before governmental bodies, counsel them on public regulations and assist them when they suffer journalistic or political attack, the Council's innovations may provide the foundation community with many valuable precedents. Indeed with some expansion of function and staff, the Council, as presently organized, could well become the body to provide the foundation community with such services.

NOTES—CHAPTER 10

1. *The Foundation Directory*, 3rd Edition, p. 650.
2. For a brief outline history, see Rich, *Community Foundations in the United States and Canada, 1914-1961* (New York, 1961), pp. 9-13. The most recent such report on community foundations entitled *1968 Status Report on Community Foundations* is available at the Council on Foundations, New York.
3. *The Investment Policies of Foundations*, p. 148.
4. *The Foundation Directory*, 3rd Edition, p. 27.
5. Rich, *op. cit.*, pp. 41, 44.
6. *Ibid.*, pp. 48, 50, 59.
7. The article appears in *Foundation News* (July-August, 1971), pp. 137 *ff*.
8. See the Foundation's *1968 Annual Report*, p. 12.
9. See, for example, *Proceedings*, 20th Annual Conference of the Council on Foundations, Inc., held at New Orleans, April 9-11, 1969, mimeographed publication of the Council, New York, New York.

Chapter 11

THE DEMAND FOR REFORM AND
GOVERNMENTAL INTERVENTION

ALTHOUGH THERE IS an ever-present possibility that the federal government might regulate foundations by conferring or withdrawing their tax exemption, Congress rarely exploited that possibility during the first half of the century. As we have already noted, foundations were regulated to a limited extent as early as the 1930s when they were restricted from trying to influence legislation as well as from participating in political campaigns in behalf of particular candidates. Tax exemption was available to a foundation "no susbtantial part of the activ-

ities of which is carrying on propaganda or otherwise attempting to influence legislation, and which does not participate in,
or intervene in (including the publishing or distributing of
statements), any political campaign on behalf of any candidate
for public office." In practice the prohibition was against outright lobbying or advocacy of pending legislation. This was
softened by the requirement that, for a foundation to be
penalized by loss of tax exemption, a "substantial part" of its
total annual expenditure had to be allocated to advocating
legislation or lobbying. Thus some undetermined amount of
money still could be so used without penalty.

Not until 1950, however, was there any additional regulation of foundations of any consequence. This followed revela-
tions that foundations were being used as tax shelters for
business, a practice exemplified by Textron, Inc., a New England
textile firm, which had exploited for its own ends the assets
and tax-exempt income of several controlled foundations.[1]
In addition to forbidding foundations from making unreason-
able accumulations of income at the expense of grants to
charity, a provision on which I have already commented,*
that legislation introduced three other reforms, each of which
was meant to prevent exploitation of a foundation for the
private advantage of those who controlled it. The first of
the reforms was directed against "unrelated" business activity
by a foundation. The Treasury was directed to deny exemption to any foundation which, though it might dispense some
charity, was also engaged directly in the conduct of a business
that had no substantial relation to the purpose for which the
foundation had secured its exemption. The second reform was
an extension of the first. It sought to discourage a foundation
which had been denied tax exemption for a business it ran
directly, from establishing a "feeder" corporation, that is, a
nominally independent but "wholly owned" foundation corporation which could take over and manage a business and

* See p. 96.

direct all its earnings to the foundation's coffers. Congress decreed that, if such a corporation were established, its profits would be taxed in exactly the same manner as the profits of any business.

The third and most important of the 1950 reforms sought to discourage the more obvious forms of self-dealing on the part of foundation managers, that is, dealings between a foundation and those who control it, the cause of so much abuse of foundations. An example of self-dealing would be a loan by the foundation to a business both of which were controlled by the same persons. At the time, the Treasury had wanted Congress to forbid all forms of self-dealing. Though the House agreed with the Treasury's position, the Senate insisted upon, and in conference secured, the substitution of another —a so-called "arms-length"—policy that actually permitted self-dealing provided it was carried on according to terms and conditions that were deemed to be "reasonable," "adequate," and "fair" in the business world. Thus a family-controlled foundation could still make loans to the donor, members of his family, or associates provided the interest rate was reasonable and security was offered that conformed to commercial standards. The foundation could also continue to provide a donor's family members, or his associates, compensation for services, provided the compensation was not excessive; the foundation could make services—for example, a scholarship— available to such persons provided that in doing so they were treated as all other persons might have been treated; the foundation could purchase securities from such persons or sell them securities provided the terms of the transaction conformed to market or "going" values; and the foundation could engage in other commercial or financial transactions with them, provided the transactions did not result in diverting foundation income or property to them without adequate recompense to the foundation.[2]

One of the chief complainants about the 1950 legislation was the Treasury itself. It objected especially to the terms

of the arms-length policy on self-dealing upon which the
Senate had insisted. As a somewhat realistic Treasury critic
observed, "the arms involved may both belong to the same
person, who is both donor and trustee;" [3] and such a bio-
logical-legal allusion was scarcely calculated to make things
easy for any sleuth who hoped to identify the parties to a
contract involving the foundation. Moreover, in several cases
in which the courts were called upon to interpret the legislation, resulting decisions were less than sympathetic to sanctions deemed essential by the Treasury if the arms-length
regulations were to be effective.[4]

Nevertheless, though the need for supplementary legislation became rather obvious, Congress refrained from acting
on the matter for almost two decades. The legislative changes
in 1964, affecting application of the unlimited deduction to
foundations, was scarcely a major or even an entirely relevant
development. When, in 1969, it did get around to considering
proposals that culminated in the foundation provisions of the
Tax Reform Act of that year, the numerous examples of the
failure of previous regulatory efforts offered by such critics
as Representative Patman [5] had brought the public attitude
towards foundations to its nadir. As a result, some of the
proposals which received serious consideration by congressional committees concerned with the new legislation seemed
less like therapy to cure the patient and more like injections
by embalmers to prepare the deceased for interment. Indeed
if, contrary to their traditions and ways of presenting their
case to the public, the foundations had themselves not finally
gone to Congress and indulged in an effort to "influence
legislation," the regulations included in the Tax Reform Act
of 1969 would have come close to ending foundations, especially if the proposed forty-year limit on any foundation's
existence had been left in the law. As it was, the foundations
did succeed in "cooling" the more extreme-minded legislators
and the Act, as it emerged from the congressional conference
towards the end of December, could still be regarded as

reform legislation rather than as legislation threatening the very existence of foundations.

Besides imposing the four percent tax on foundations, nudging them to liquidate controlling interests in corporations and businesses, and requiring them to make a minimum payout to charity—matters which we have already discussed at length —the Tax Reform Act had two principal objectives. The first was to discourage exploitation of a foundation for the private economic advantage of those who control it. The second was to expand limitations on the philanthropic discretion of foundations particularly in areas deemed politically sensitive. It is these two aspects of the Act which will be discussed in the remainder of this Chapter. It might be added that internal organization and the management of foundations, subjects with which this volume chiefly deals, were ignored in the legislation except as they incidentally affected these two and other objectives of the legislation.

To discourage the manipulation of foundations for the personal advantage of those who controlled them, the new law incorporated the recommendations, so often reiterated by Treasury people, that, instead of merely interposing an "arms-length" requirement on self-dealing between a family or other type foundation and donors, contributors, and other related persons, such transactions be prohibited. A considerable list of potential types of self-dealers was drawn up that identifies "disqualified persons," that is, people who would be disqualified from entering into dealings with the foundation with which they are connected. Among others, these persons include any substantial contributor (anyone who has donated as much as 5 thousand dollars to the foundation in *any* year), such as the family donor or members of his family, a person who has a major interest in a business or trust which is a substantial contributor to the foundation, the business or trust itself under certain circumstances, and trustees and officials of the foundation.[6] These "disqualified persons" cannot engage in transactions with the foundation that involve selling, leasing, or exchanging property, lending money, extending credit, or furnishing goods or services. The prohibitions are enforceable by tax penalties.

The provisions of the 1969 legislation against self-dealing do not, however, make it legally impossible for a founding family member, or other "disqualified person" to continue to operate a foundation. He may continue to do this and he may even receive compensation for his services if the compensation is not "excessive." He may also be provided with services by the foundation provided these same kinds of services are furnished to all without discrimination. Congress clearly did not intend to prevent the creator of a family foundation from controlling its operations but merely to prevent him from exploiting it for private economic gain. The founder of a foundation can still give his money to a foundation and then, through his control of the foundation, determine who shall receive grants from the foundation, that is, give the money away a second time.

Let us turn now to the second major regulatory feature of the 1969 legislation, namely, that directed at a type of foundation philanthropic policy, which had received increasing criticism during the 1950s and the 1960s. The criticism had been expressed in some of the testimony heard by the first of the three congressional committees, that led by Representative Cox. It had dominated the testimony and set the tone of the report of the second of the three committees, led by Representative Reece. The criticism consisted of charges that foundation money supported extremist causes, especially of the left; that indirectly, if not directly, it influenced the fate of issues at the polls and before legislative assemblies and administrative bodies; that sometimes it directly aided candidates for public office; and that it financed research the results of which were politically slanted or, in any case, of no social worth.

Although, happily, the 1969 legislation did not try to satisfy the more extreme among the critics—such as those who demanded that foundation support of allegedly leftist persons or causes be prohibited—it did establish new categorical limitations on the purposes for which a foundation may make grants, and some of these limitations carry distinct overtones that are contrary to the liberal point of view.

The new legislation has strengthened earlier limitations on efforts by foundations to influence public policy. It prohibits *any* expenditure for advocacy or lobbying. The foundation could lose its exemption for making any expenditure for this purpose and may be penalized further with a tax of 10 percent of the actual expenditure. A tax of 2.5 percent of the expenditure may also be levied upon the individual foundation executive who knowingly sanctioned it.[7] Moreover, the term "influencing legislation" was made to include efforts to "affect the opinion of the general public or any segment thereof" and efforts to communicate privately with a legislator, legislative employee, or any person involved in the legislative process.[8] All this constitutes a far broader prohibition of advocacy and lobbying than before 1969.

Similar prohibitions and penalties are directed toward other forms of "political activity." These include foundation support of any effort "to influence the outcome of any specific public election," including voter-registration drives. Apparently an intention to exert "influence" does not have to be supported by evidence; an allegation that the effort was made is all that is required to bring the foundation into question under the new law. To be sure, the law specifies formal exemption from the operation of these prohibitions to preserve the traditional non-partisan educational and informational services of organizations like the National League of Women Voters and the Southern Regional Council; but the rather onerous conditions under which such exemptions are to be granted seem to promise less than a full guarantee that these organizations may operate as they have in the past.[9]

To make more certain that foundations keep out of "public-policy areas," the architects of the new legislation have even gone so far as to restrict the access of foundation staff members to government bureaucrats, apparently in the belief that unrestricted access will tempt and perhaps contaminate the foundation or the bureaucrat. Like the donors of foundations and certain other persons mentioned earlier, high governmental officials have been singled out and labeled "disqualified persons." High appointive or elective governmental officials may not even be compensated for attending a foundation-financed seminar or discussion group, and they may not be reimbursed for all of their out-of-pocket expenses unless the foundation involved is willing to incur the penalties prescribed for self-dealing. As the congressional sponsors explained these prohibitions, they are intended to "minimize the possibility of improper influencing of the attitude, or conduct, of such policy-making level officials." [10]

Foundations also are restricted in the new law in making grants to individuals. Some legislators became concerned by the political implications of certain direct, non-categorical, grants which a major foundation had made to departing members of the entourage of the late Senator Robert F. Kennedy. The legislators demanded that such direct grants be given special attention in the new legislation. As a result, foundations can make grants to individuals without restriction only if they are a part of a regularly administered scholarship or fellowship program. All others can be made only by securing Treasury approval in advance and they must also be made on a "nondiscriminatory" basis. In addition, the new legislation requires that something tangible emanate from such a grant to an individual—at least that a report be made public.

Earlier I noted that the Treasury is called upon to approve and monitor a grant to any organization that is not recognized as a charity under the revenue code. The foundation must report to the Treasury and convince it that the grant is for a "tax-exempt purpose" and must also secure reports regularly from the recipient of the grant and make certain that the recipient is keeping within the limitations of the grant and fulfilling its purpose. Obviously the Treasury can withdraw exemption for cause at any point. Failure of the foundation to fulfill its obligations satisfactorily can result in the imposition of sizable tax fines upon the foundation and the responsible foundation executive or trustee. [11]

Encouraging foundations to monitor and appraise grants, evaluate the results, and make appropriate reports are among my recommendations to improve foundation management. However, to place an already overworked Internal Revenue Service into the business of approving grants to individuals and institutions, and appraising results, is probably not the most efficient use of Service personnel. Neither is such a policy one that will encourage initiative on the part of a foundation staff or preserve its independence.

On balance these regulations affecting philanthropic policy will have a detrimental effect. They will make it more difficult to recruit or retain competent administrators and trustees partly because of the personal tax liabilities involved in the new penalties and partly because foundation service will be less challenging. The regulations can also force a foundation out of almost any field that has even a remote connection with the organized political and legislative process. They threaten the long-sustained and effective efforts which foundations have been making to assist the Negro and other minorities to realize their civil and political rights. They will weaken foundation efforts to promote public education and understanding of the issues of the day, for example, issues such as conservation, hunger and malnutrition, the dangers of the use of tobacco, the educational impact on children of certain types of radio and television programs, and the problems of violence and corruption. They will discourage efforts by any but the largest and most influential foundations to take sides on any controversial issue relating to social behavior, or even to scientific research or social or technological demonstration since all such issues are potentially subject to governmental policy and hence grist for political debate at some governmental level. On some great issues, for example, any of a series of proposals to control and impede degradation of the environment, issues on which private business can apparently take a stand before governmental bodies and charge the resulting cost to business expense, foundations, which may be the only agencies financially capable of presenting and defending the public interest, may have to stay silent or be penalized. The effect may well be a kind of imbalance in public opinion detrimental to popular government and the values of a democratic society.

The potential impact of the broad areas of regulation will become apparent only as the Treasury expands interpretations and offers appropriate guide lines for the enforcement of the Tax Reform Act, and as the courts interpret them in cases as they arise. The probable impact of the regulation, however, is already reasonably clear. There is little doubt that the 1969 legislation will overcome some of the less desirable ways that directors manipulate foundations for nonphilanthropic ends. It is also fairly obvious that, unless tempered by a relaxed administration, the expanded public control of foundation philanthropic discretion will interfere with policy-making by the foundations. The result may be to encourage foundations to consider only conventional and "safe" philanthropy, inhibit innovation, and discourage the more enterprising and forward-looking individuals from entering upon foundation employment. As one observer suggested to me recently, the effect may be to make an already conservative institution even more conservative.

NOTES—CHAPTER 11

1. *Hearings before a Subcommittee of the Senate Committee on Interstate and Foreign Commerce*—Closing of Nashua, N.H. Mills—1948, 80th Congress, 2nd Session, and *Yale Law Journal*, LIX, 1950, pp. 59 and 1121. See also Andrews, *Patman and Foundations: Review and Assessment* (New York, 1968), p. 1.
2. Section 681 of the Internal Revenue Code of 1954.
3. *Treasury Department Report on Private Foundations* (Washington, Government Printing Office, February, 1965), p. 181.
4. See also comment in Fremont-Smith, *op. cit.*, p. 183.
5. *Hearings before Subcommittee No. 1 on Foundations* (Mr. Patman's Subcommittee on Foundations), Select Committee on Small Business, House of Representatives, 88th Congress, 2nd Session, Washington, Government Printing Office, 1964, p. 65. See also, the issue of *Ramparts Magazine*, cited earlier, and Lundberg, *The Rich and the Super Rich* (New York, 1968), pp. 382-432.
6. Act, Section 101b; Code, Sections 4946 and 4941.
7. Again the penalties are staggered with three levels, the second one being 100% on the foundation and 50% on the executive, Act, Section 101b; Code, Section 4945.
8. Act, Section 101b; Code, Section 4945.
9. See, for example, testimony of American Civil Liberties Union, in Part A, *Testimony etc.*, Tax Reform Act of 1969, H.R. 13270, 91st Congress, 1st Session, Washington, Government Printing Office, 1969, pp. 63 ff. For the conditions see Act, Section 101b; Code, Section 4945(f).
10. *Report of the Committee on Ways and Means*, to accompany H.R. 13270, 91st Congress, 1st Session, Washington, Government Printing Office, 1969, p. 23.
11. Act, Section 101b; Code, Section 4945 (d) (3) (4) (g) and (h).

Chapter 12

RESPONSE OF THE FOUNDATION
COMMUNITY TO REGULATION

THE IMMEDIATE REACTION of those involved with foundations to the provisions of the Tax Reform Act of 1969 was a mixed one. A few foundation heads denounced the provisions in their entirety. Their denunciation was inspired, in part, by the failure of the congressional leadership to distinguish between the good and bad foundations. Lumping them together, they insisted, had led the legislators to establish some regulations that were unnecessary and even dangerous for the conforming foundations. Also, they said, this had the effect of destroying public confidence in all foundations.

The great majority of foundation spokesmen were more moderate and more selective in their immediate appraisal of the legislation. Almost all of them felt that the effort to eliminate self-dealing and to overcome exploitation of a foundation for nonphilanthropic purposes was commendable. A lesser number approved the payout provision and the effort to secure reduction of family holdings in foundation portfolios. Very few approved the 4 percent tax on foundations, or the restrictions on foundation philanthropic policy, or the special sanctions which may now be levied against foundation personnel. These feelings of the foundation community were rather appropriately summarized in comments offered by the heads of some of the larger and more active foundations at a press conference held shortly after the President signed the Tax Reform Act. The new legislation, said these spokesmen, was not as bad as it might have been and "on balance" was even "good." [1]

In the period since the adoption of the Act, however, there has been little evidence that foundations may take a more constructive stance on the issue of reform and themselves assume the initiative. Some have sought to enlist public sympathy for the elimination of the 4 percent tax.[2] Others have tried to whittle down the payout provisions of the Act, an effort which incidentally, as we have already noted, has met with some success.[3]

Still others have advanced claims, first made in the middle sixties,[4] that the states are the appropriate regulatory agencies of foundations. Some of those who made such claims sincerely believed this to be the case but others really believed that the states would be more flexible regulatory agencies than the Treasury and that, because of this, foundations could escape from growing federal regulation. They argued that the states created virtually all foundations and hence ought to determine their privileges and responsibilities; the congressional power of regulation, they held, was merely an indirect power, derived from the direct power over the revenue.

It is possible that these arguments may induce some of the states to expand and improve the supervision of foundations. One or two, for example, New York, have already done so. Furthermore, they may be encouraged by the Tax Reform Act itself which instructs the Treasury to inform the appropriate state official, such as the attorney general or tax officer, of the withdrawal of federal tax exemption from any organization or the levying of tax fines on any foundation.[5] However, the idea that the states might contain the Treasury's growing regulatory power is hard to believe, for this is an era of high federal taxes and a virtual federal monopoly of tax sources. Foundations must have federal tax exemption and their donors must be allowed tax deductions, which only the federal agencies can give. Hence Congress and the Treasury are hardly likely to forgo the power to police and regulate that arises out of the power to confer or withhold exemption and deductibility.

Actually, federal regulation is more likely to increase, whatever the states may do. The first reason is that increasingly sophisticated sanctions have been made available to the Treasury for policing foundations which only encourage greater control. Originally only one sanction could be resorted to, and that was denial of exemption. Since 1969, as I have already noted, the Treasury can levy penalty taxes both on the foundation and foundation official. Penalty taxes do not seriously penalize philanthropy as does withdrawal of exemption, and the Treasury may accordingly be more willing to resort to them.

A second reason why federal regulation is likely to hold its own and probably expand at the expense of the states is the difficulty of establishing common standards among the states. A few states are forward looking; a great many more are indifferent to the problem of appropriate regulation and lax in enforcing the standards that do exist.[6] This variation could work a hardship especially upon the more active foundations which operate nationally and even internationally.

Still a third reason why any proposed return of the control of foundations to the states is unrealistic is that many of those interested in foundation reform look to Washington rather than to the states for satisfaction. This tendency is illustrated by one of the major recommendations of the Peterson Commission, a private group headed by the president (at the time) of the Bell and Howell Company, that studied foundations in 1969 and made recommendations to Congress. The Commission suggested that a "philanthropic policy board" be established, consisting of ten or fifteen members of which the minority would come from the government. The policy board was to be charged with continuous study of foundations and to make annual reports to Congress and the President. These reports would provide the basis for further legislation and public policy towards foundations.[7]

Occasionally reactions of the foundation community to the 1969 legislation were more constructive. Possibly the most constructive, at least for the longer term, was the development of plans for a national foundation agency. Initial steps were taken shortly after the bill was signed into law. A committee of five distinguished foundation heads or former foundation officials, headed by John Gardner, former president of the Carnegie Corporation, was asked to explore the possibility of "a more rational framework for the field, and . . . a stronger structure." [8] Nominally, the committee's sponsors were The Foundation Center, the Council on Foundations, and the National Council on Philanthropy. The moving force, however, was a group of leading foundation executives who had been meeting prior to the hearings on the tax measure from time to time to consider common interests. Because the Tax Reform Act had made the special concession to exempt foundations from its lobbying provisions when they pleaded their own institutional case before legislative and other governmental bodies,[9] the special committee recommended that a kind of national foundation council, not unlike a trade association, should be established. This could serve as spokesman for foundations before the government and the public.

When first announced, plans for the contemplated agency were quite ambitious. It was proposed to consolidate, or at least "co-ordinate" under it existing foundation agencies, that is, The Foundation Center and the Council on Foundations. (As I have noted earlier, the former is intended to be a reference and information service agency for the general public; the latter is an agency to serve constituent foundations.) The consolidated agencies would direct all activities that concern foundations as a group; that is, they would not restrict themselves to representing foundations before legislatures and other governmental bodies, and to public relations, but they also would provide general information and reference services, and even research on foundation policies and activities.

At this writing, the proposed agency has not been set up. If and when it is, it will probably depart considerably from the original blueprint. Already it seems to have been agreed that the objectivity of reference and information services might be questioned if brought too closely under the jurisdiction of an agency so directly controlled by the foundations. At any rate most of these services will continue to be carried out by The Foundation Center which, at least for the time being, will continue on an autonomous basis and not be merged with the Council on Foundations. The latter will also continue and expand its role as a service agency for all types of foundations. Research into foundation operations and practices will apparently continue to be done by certain foundations that have specialized in it in the past and by the universities. However, if the proposed national agency is eventually established, even in this less ambitious form, or because of it, the agency, if well led and properly managed, could undoubtedly contribute to the elimination of some of the distrust and misunderstanding of foundations that has become endemic in governmental and other circles in recent years.

Foundations have also been trying to overcome some of their deficiencies in other areas and the new legislation has probably given a fillip to such efforts. One has been an effort to reduce the traditional isolation of foundations and those who operate them. By means of occasional university-sponsored forums and *ad hoc* or regularly scheduled regional and national meetings, foundation administrators are discovering new opportunities to take counsel with one another and with "outside" experts. Occasions of this sort are exploited not merely to protect the group interests of foundations and people who are identified with them, but to identify more creative opportunities in philanthropy and projects that involve more than one foundation. Such occasions also provide valuable seminars on improving foundation management.

Progress has also been made in closing the "information gap" between the public and foundations by publishing *The Foundation Directory*, first through The Foundation Center and Russell Sage Foundation in 1960. It has reached its fourth edition and now contains basic information on more than 5000 foundations. Directories of foundations outside the United States, notably those in Western Europe and Latin America, have also been published by Russell Sage Foundation. *Foundation News*, a bimonthly publication, introduced by The Foundation Center, but continued since 1971 by the Council on Foundations, is the source of much current information about foundations. In recent years, also, Russell Sage Foundation, usually alone but sometimes in cooperation with The Foundation Center, has issued scholarly publications about foundations related to philanthropic policy, foundation investment policies, the foundation trustee and administrator, the public accountability of foundations, the position of foundations under the law, and foundation relations with government, both state and national.[10]

Hence in their response to recent criticism and federal regulation the foundations have some pluses. What they have done or are seeking to do by working together to put their house in order is modestly impressive. Not so impressive, however, are the responses made by foundations individually. Indeed in respect to the principal concern of this volume, namely, internal management, the response has so far been disappointing. In the study of foundation staffing, to which attention was called earlier, there was little indication that the new legislation had noticeably modified the traditional antipathy to hiring professional help that the majority of even the sizable foundations exhibit, although some of the wealthier foundations, which up to now have operated without employees of executive calibre, are beginning to hire a few such persons. But the persons hired probably will be chiefly competent to cope with the new federal regulations concerning payout, tax reporting, and other things. Rarely will they be specialists in developing program.

Indeed, many who reported to the study felt that, because of the limitations on philanthropic policy in the new legislation, the legislation may well discourage program staffing.[11] Without such people, it is unlikely that many of the weaknesses in internal administration such as delays in processing requests for grants, failure to explain the foundation program to potential applicants for assistance, ineffective appraisal and monitoring of projects and programs, and failure to provide the public with adequate reports on foundation activities, are likely to be remedied. Absence of competent program staff discourages innovation and creativity in foundation programming and militates against improvement in the overall philanthropic performance.

The lack of concern for improving internal management is also indicated by the fate of a recent plan to establish a code of operating standards for foundations. A precedent for such a code had been provided in the 1960s when F. Emerson Andrews, then president of The Foundation Center, drew up a list of standards and circulated it among a few individuals. His proposed code drew a cool reception at the time; but, as criticisms of foundations mounted, it was considered more favorably. A special committee of experienced and respected foundation administrators, brought together under the auspices of The Foundation Center, the Council on Foundations, and the National Council on Philanthropy, drew up a revised code in 1969.[12] It was anticipated that, in due course, a permanent committee on foundation operating standards would be set up to enforce the code. The permanent committee, it was suggested, might be called upon to evaluate foundations at their request, publish the names of those foundations that met proposed standards of operation, and even publish the names of those foundations which, after complaint and investigation, were found to be derelict in observing the standards. In time, the permanent committee might have become a sort of "certification" agency among foundations, useful in encouraging foundations to police themselves. It might also have served as a means by which the normally higher standards of conduct and management of the more advanced foundations could have been used to influence the more backward members of the foundation fraternity.

Several of the proposed standards, for example, avoidance of self-dealing, a respectable minimum payout to charity, and improved reporting on operations, were incorporated, at least in part, in the Tax Reform Act. This fact may have been a principal reason why the code was never adopted, as well as the fact that it won few friends among boards of trustees and chief executives of even the more advanced foundations. In any event, after a brief flare of publicity, the proposal disappeared from the foundation community's agenda. With it disappeared also any serious immediate collective concern for improving operations and management in the individual foundations.

In summary, then, the response of foundations to recent criticisms, and to federal regulation of unprecedented scope and severity, has, on balance, been disappointing. Some constructive steps, already underway when the legislation was passed, have been given new impetus. The legislation also seems to have persuaded the foundation constituency to seek a more visible and more cohesive instrument to defend its collective interests. On the other hand, considerable energy seems to have been expended in rather negative criticisms of the legislation, in efforts to soften its terms, and even in encouraging the substitution of state for federal regulation. As respects the basic issue of internal reform, moreover, there is little evidence of any constructive response. Foundations have remained relatively indifferent to the need to improve management and to recruit the staffs essential to high operating standards.

Given the fact that many foundations felt their very existence was in jeopardy, it is perhaps not surprising that they should have given priority to improving their collective relations with government and public and ignored or given second place to their managerial and administrative weaknesses. On the other hand, if foundations are really concerned about their preservation, they will find that public relations and image-making will scarcely suffice. For foundations, especially, any effective prescription for survival requires facing up to institutional weaknesses and improving standards of internal operation and management. Continuing to ignore those shortcomings can only raise doubts that foundations are in fact the private institutions for public welfare that they profess to be or that they are really serious about countering the ministrations of those who would make them only a memory.

NOTES—CHAPTER 12

1. *New York Times* (January 11, 1970).
2. See, for example, The Henry Luce Foundation Inc., *Report for 1970*, p. 12.
3. See p. 98.

4. On the general subject, see testimony of Dana S. Creel and supplementary statement by Dean William C. Warren in *Additional Written Statement, etc., on Treasury Department Report on Private Foundations,* February 2, 1965, submitted to Committee on Ways and Means, 89th Congress, 1st Session, Vol. II, Washington, Government Printing Office, 1965, pp. 744-746 and 746-758.

5. Act, Section 101 (e); Code, Section 6104 (c).

6. Fremont-Smith, *op. cit.,* pp. 50, 240-241. See generally Chaps. vi-ix inclusive.

7. See *Testimony to be Received Wednesday, October 22, 1969,* Topic, Foundations, by Senate Finance Committee, on Tax Reform Act, H.R. 13270, 91st Congress, 1st Session, Washington, Government Printing Office, 1969, p. 90. For final report of the Peterson Commission, see *Report and Recommendations of the Commission on Foundations and Private Philanthropy* (Chicago, Illinois, 1970).

8. Comment of Alan Pifer in *Foundations and the Tax Reform Act of 1969* (The Foundation Center, New York, 1970), p. 45.

9. Act, Section 101 b; Code, Section 4945 (e).

10. The following is the rather impressive bibliography of relevant titles: F. Emerson Andrews, *Philanthropic Giving,* 1950; *Philanthropic Foundations,* 1956; *Legal Instruments of Foundations,* 1958, and *Foundations: Twenty Viewpoints,* 1965; Frank M. Andrews, *A Study of Company-Sponsored Foundations,* 1960; Fremont-Smith, *Foundations and Government,* 1965; Harrison and Andrews, *American Foundations for Social Welfare,* 1946; Kiger, *Operating Principles of the Larger Foundations,* 1954; Nelson, *The Investment Policies of Foundations,* 1967; Taylor, *Public Accountability of Foundations and Charitable Trusts,* 1953; Young and Moore, *Trusteeship and the Management of Foundations,* 1969; and Zurcher and Dustan, *The Foundation Administrator,* 1972.

11. See Zurcher and Dustan, *The Foundation Administrator* (New York, 1972), pp. 35-36.

12. An announcement of the plan appears in *Foundation News* (November-December, 1969), pp. 312 ff.

Chapter 13

DOES THE FOUNDATION HAVE
A FUTURE?

CAN THE FOUNDATION SURVIVE if it succeeds in placing its house
in order and improves its management? There are those who
believe that the foundation as an institution may continue to
exist but that no particular foundation ought to continue beyond a number of years, say, one or two generations. They
consider the perpetual existence, normally guaranteed a foundation, whether a corporation or trust, to be wrong in principle because no large aggregation of wealth ought to be
given a life that continues generation after generation. For

166   THE MANAGEMENT OF AMERICAN FOUNDATIONS

them it is also bad policy because, if foundations continue indefinitely, they are likely to perpetuate outmoded ideas or, at any rate, fail to adjust their sights to new needs. Some founders of foundations like Falk, Couzens, Rosenwald, James, and Fleischmann, have had such doubts and have either ordered their trustees to bring the foundation to an end after a term of years or liquidate when they saw fit. In part, it was this attitude that prompted certain legislators to suggest the 40-year limitation on the life of any foundation during the debate on the Tax Reform Act of 1969.

The issue of survival is, however, much broader. It concerns all foundations. It raises the question whether foundations, as a class of institution, have outlived their usefulness and hence are expendable. If there is any real threat to the continued existence of foundations, aside from that arising from their conduct and management, it lies in the answer to this question rather than to the one on perpetuities.

Critics supporting the view that foundations are no longer useful are impressed with the possibility that, in a relatively few years, the comprehensive welfare type of government which has evolved in this century may absorb all the functions of the foundation and make it superfluous. Government at various levels has almost completely taken over most of the historical functions of the foundation concerned with alleviating distress and aiding the indigent. Since the end of World War II, it has also begun to take over responsibility for many of the "newer" foundation activities in research and experimental programs that the larger, general-purpose foundations finance and the support of established medical, scientific, educational, and cultural institutions. Should this process of governmental "aggrandizement" continue, say these critics, the functions of the foundation would be preempted.

Moreover, as government moves to support these programs for which the foundation spends its funds, government would logically begin to covet the foundation's untaxed wealth. The foundations' 25 billion dollars of assets and 1.5

billion dollars of annual expenditures are, to be sure, a pittance when compared with the 230 billion dollar federal budget and the outlays of state and local governments. Nevertheless, as the recent legislation taxing foundations indicates, even the foundations' limited resources might be taken away by extending the existing tax on foundations to a point where it would effectively eliminate foundation resources.

The idea that government may supplant foundations is a plausible one but there are various reasons why it is not likely to happen. First, no matter how much governments may invade areas hitherto reserved for private foundation philanthropy, the demands on such philanthropy do not appear to diminish. In a civilization of growing cultural sophistication, in which the horizon of the material expectations of the citizenry is constantly widening, no public budget, however generous, seems to be able to keep up with changing and expanding social demands. Second, changing priorities and old-fashioned economic recessions often force the government to reduce the funding of established projects and programs. The people who conduct these projects must then turn to private sources, including foundations, to take up the public budgetary slack. Third, the government may indeed be tempted to increase the tax on foundations and make life financially difficult for them, but the more knowledgeable counsellors on the public revenue are likely to advise that, though the total annual contribution of foundations to charity cannot rise much above 1 percent of the federal government's annual budget, that contribution would still be larger than the amount that would be yielded if government were to indulge in severe taxation of foundations and seek to substitute the resulting yield for the contribution that normally flows to charity from foundations.

But the case for the survival of the foundation is not merely a dollar-and-cents matter—the case does not rest solely on what the foundation can contribute to charity. Another reason why foundations will probably continue to exist, a reason more important than the financial resources it contributes, are the unique advantages that the foundation enjoys over government as each seeks to discharge its role in promoting social and cultural progress.

The first of these advantages is of a logistical nature. A major foundation can, if it will, and if it is desirable, expedite the mobilization of resources and manpower and thus reduce the interval between the design and operational stages of a project. Unlike most of the research and investigative branches of government which move rather sedately and whose funds are normally earmarked for specific purposes, and often strictly categorized as to use, a foundation can move quickly and its funds are relatively unencumbered. As noted earlier, some foundations can even expedite their own action in funding an accepted project by allowing officers or staff members to make discretionary grants of a magnitude sufficient for at least the exploratory or preparatory phases of a project. Also, whatever their own staff weaknesses, at least the great foundations are often more successful than agencies of government in finding the best men and women for a specific assignment and in persuading them to undertake that assignment.

A second and even more valuable advantage a foundation enjoys is its relative freedom from organized social pressure. Unlike governmental agencies, the foundation has no organized body of voters to please, no elections to win, and, normally, no lobbyists to withstand. The absence of any special constituencies which it must please may make the foundation vulnerable to attack; and the foundation itself may abuse its freedom from the pressure of public opinion. But when that freedom is exercised wisely and with a sense of dedication to long-term social interests, it offers the foundation a most important advantage over governmental action.

Because of this freedom the foundation is under fewer constraints than government, or probably any other institution except possibly the university, in promoting pure scientific research, in underwriting projects that look to fundamental discovery rather than to immediate social advantage, and in supporting the young and unknown scholar rather than the scholar with a sizable reputation. Nor, except for an occasional hostile editorial or a congressional committee, is it hampered in investigating the most unpopular or the most sensitive of issues, be it birth control, the fluoridation of water, improvement of the jury system, or sex mores and sex behavior. (At least this was true until the criticism of the 1960s and the enactment of the reform legislation of 1969 created a less-favorable climate for foundations.) Moreover, as I noted in Chapter 8, the independence of the foundation, even from its own government, is also very consequential when a foundation seeks to carry out a program outside the United States. Foreign governments may accept or request the aid of a foundation when, for various political reasons, they cannot accept aid from the foundation's own government.

Just how valuable these advantages of the foundation are may become more apparent if we provide a brief agenda of some of the problems that will press for solution during the decade of the 1970s. They are problems the consideration of which can benefit from these foundation attributes, that is both the capacity to make quick and flexible responses and the foundation's independence. Hence they invite foundation intervention and suggest that a foundation, rather than government, assume primary, or at least preliminary, responsibility for their consideration. The agenda will be directed primarily to the more mature intermediate and general-purpose foundations; but it will include opportunities available to the smaller family, company-sponsored and community foundations, which traditionally engage in supportive philanthropy. In any case they will be problems designed to illustrate the continued need for the special institutional advantages of the foundation. They are not a comprehensive agenda for future foundation activity.

Among problems on any such agenda, high priority should be given to reforming and updating the government itself.

Particularly is this true of Congress, with its seniority system, its much too dominant committee chairmen, its procedural maze, and its "third chamber" of lobbyists. Taken together, these frequently defeat the will of majorities and far too often make democracy a laughing stock. In need of attention, also, is the Presidency. Partly the need is to make it more responsive to public opinion, especially in its conduct of foreign affairs, but more effective ways must be found to keep the President and his staff from being overwhelmed by the sheer bureaucratic size of modern government and to keep them free to exercise the informed public and legislative leadership which contemporary society requires. To cope with such matters, a properly managed foundation can be a less prejudiced, more independent, and hence more objective instrument than some governmental agency, especially in the politically sensitive areas of investigation and appraisal.*

Other organizations are no less in need of attention than the governmental. Corporate business is high on the list because of its questionable tendency to merge the most disparate kinds of production and services, its growing and often superfluous bureaucracies, its increasing dependence on public loans and grants, and its increasingly irresponsible attitude towards the consumer. Organized labor is another candidate because of its inability or unwillingness to discard the outmoded and socially intolerable policy of strikes and confrontations and to seek instead new ways to achieve reasonable demands. Still another candidate are the universities which are experiencing increasing difficulty in governing and financing themselves and in determining how their role in education and research can effectively meet contemporary needs. These institutional weaknesses present an especially appropriate challenge to imaginative foundation leadership that is willing to invest even limited resources of money and talent.

---

* It is possible, of course, that the regulatory provisions of the 1969 Tax Reform Act, already discussed, will discourage foundation concern with governmental institutions.

Equally high on an agenda appropriate to foundations is their possible support of efforts to evaluate and control powerful social forces being released by science and technology, and in establishing priorities for science and technology themselves—in short, in planning the future. Congressional and departmental committees and presidential advisory agencies have made real progress in implementing this process of national planning during the past generation. So, too, have various committees of such private organizations as the National Academy of Sciences and the American Council on Education. In a complex and fast-changing technologically-oriented society, planning national goals and establishing priorities are indispensable if we wish to provide intelligent and understandable options for democratic electorates and representative assemblies and prevent democracy, as a form of government, from degenerating into a mere façade. More intimate and more extensive foundation involvement in the process would lend that process a degree of impartiality that could help to insure its substantive integrity and its public acceptance.

Above and beyond the problems of the social structure itself is that all too characteristic and all too pervasive problem of the late 20th century, that of trying to reidentify the individual with society. As sociologists have frequently observed, the institutions and organized processes of society have become so bureaucratized and depersonalized that the individual feels himself to be a social outcast or perhaps a new kind of hermit. The sense of alienation, and the consequent desire to reidentify in some constructive fashion, are obviously implicit in the revolt of youth against the "establishment," and especially in youth's vague demand for some form of "participatory democracy." Because the problem needs to be defined, because its solution is urgent, and because government and the more conventional agencies will pay little attention to it, foundations ought to take it up.

Related to this problem of reidentification, and possibly a major part of the solution to it, is to try to keep people off the economic scrapheap. As welfare rolls mount, even the most socially insensitive individual realizes that we must exploit more creatively than we have the capacity of our technology to create new vocational outlets or to expand existing ones. At the same time, we should commit ourselves to a training program commensurate with the capacity of all the unemployed and replace their mere maintenance with the satisfaction that comes from some form of socially useful and compensated work. The foundations could also consider the problems of older people. Constant inflation is eroding their savings and pensions, and the majority are condemned to exist at a sub-standard level, in a society that professes to have no use for them and merely tolerates them. They have more than a moral claim to the guarantees of whatever limited economic security they have achieved for themselves; and they, too, have a claim to continued active participation in the affairs of society. Government and private institutions are more likely to move to alleviate the condition of both of these groups only after dispassionate inquiry, at which some of the leading foundations have become especially expert, measures the problem and suggests possible solutions.

Finally in this same category of problems is that unfinished business of the fifties and sixties—satisfaction of the claims of the Negro and other minorities to first-class citizenship. Government can provide the proper legal and administrative climate and the sometimes sizable appropriations that may be required to satisfy this claim, but, as did the Carnegie Corporation when it financed Gunnar Myrdal's *An American Dilemma*, foundations can identify the many special facets of the problem of discrimination and enforced helotry, and formulate the standards society must observe in order to satisfy the minimum requirements of equal treatment. Moreover, with exploratory and other appropriate demonstration projects, foundations can provide institutional and administrative models for governmental and industrial action programs intended to assist minorities.

Beyond the problems that are more purely social, other needs exist which foundations are especially capable of satisfying. Two such needs will be mentioned as illustrations. The first is that of advancing the sophistication of the managerial art and, as the managers hopefully benefit from it themselves, extend it also to managing our social concerns. Foundations can, if they will, help importantly in encouraging the use of new quantitative tools by management and extending the managerial art, thus strengthened, to public agencies, educational institutions, scientific, medical-research, and health-care centers, and to all kinds of voluntary community-service efforts.

The second illustrative need which foundations can help to satisfy is that of accommodating the public mentality to a necessary, albeit revolutionary, change in accepted values. For example, American society is presently confronted with the necessity of substituting a concept of biological and ecological equilibrium for the popular belief that progress is characterized by uncontrolled expansion and greater size. Preservation of the natural environment and the conservation of resources, even at the expense of some immediate economic gain or technical advance, will raise relatively unprecedented issues which violate the traditional concepts of what constitutes progress. No doubt we shall encounter almost insurmountable difficulties in seeking to counter the misuse of resources, economic blight, cultural decline, social and racial discrimination, or unchecked population increase. Especially will this be so as we move to cope with the problems of the "core" cities or metropolitan areas, or even of what we still call the countryside. Again, because, unlike government, foundations are relatively free of the passions of politics and have a reputation for supporting scholarly objectivity and unbiased judgment, they have a unique opportunity to render service.

The problems appropriate for a foundation for the next decade become even more challenging outside the United States, especially in those areas which we euphemistically label "underdeveloped." As already indicated in Chapter 8, the American general-purpose foundation with an established reputation has often succeeded in initiating projects in another state which local cultural, religious, or political groups would have opposed if undertaken by the American government, or by the United Nations, or even by the foreign state itself. Economic aid to underdeveloped areas must continue to be a primary responsibility of national governments, appropriate specialized agencies of the United Nations, and regional associations of states like the European Economic Community. However, training local people for technical and managerial positions, establishing the necessary training and research institutions, helping to bend educational policy towards the physical sciences and technology, initiating plans to develop a better balance between population and resources and to rescue a nation from the hopelessness of a one-commodity export economy—these continue to offer especially attractive and appropriate projects for private foundations to undertake.

In the developing world, the highest priority will continue to attend efforts to solve the problem of human numbers. No problem is more sensitive to political and other forms of social pressure; and none is proving to be more intractable. Nevertheless, whatever the obstacles to solution, it will become imperative in the next few years to stabilize population growth rates wherever the globe is habitable and reduce them quite drastically in the globe's economically depressed parts. The alternative is scarcely acceptable. It is resigning ourselves to a world that, in a surprisingly brief period, can become one vast ghetto of six billion inhabitants, or accepting a rugged Malthusian policy of population control which exploits the fruits of the Manhattan project. Here, certainly, is a substantive area for investigation and action that could profitably consume the resources of more than one of the great American foundations during the next decade. Moreover the record of foundations' past involvement in this problem, limited though it has been, demonstrates that among all institutions, private and governmental, that have sought to cope with this sensitive subject, the foundation has the reputation of having been the most successful in undertaking pertinent research and initiating programs.

Appropriate opportunities for foundation action in the international field extend beyond the needs of developing nations. Among them will be the application of the new behavioral sciences to the solution of the problems of community and nation building; the development of insights into the managerial and technological requirements of integrating the economies of states on a regional or broadly international scale; assistance to scholarly efforts to bring about greater uniformity in private law among groups of nations and to create a body of public world law; establishment of more general standards on the civil rights of persons to be enforced by courts and administrative tribunals; and pioneering international cooperation in space and, eventually, developing an international sanction for space law. All these opportunities, however challenging, are intrinsically less important than discovering some new insights and approaches to the perennial problem of achieving political and administrative cooperation, on a global scale, for the control of burgeoning national armaments and the manufacture and trade in arms. In attacking any of these subjects, the foundations at least could clarify goals for governments and probably expedite action on their part.

From what I have said above, it is reasonable to assume that foundations are not likely to run out of worthwhile projects whatever competition they may experience from government. Indeed the opportunity to contribute their wealth and their unique institutional values to the solution of social and cultural problems is probably greater than at any time in the past. The real threat to their survival arises, therefore, not from any lack of opportunity to serve nor from a governmental takeover. The threat lies rather within the confines of the issue implicitly posed in this volume, namely, whether foundations can so order their internal operations and achieve a sufficient degree of managerial competence to develop the capability of responding successfully to the challenges that confront them. That is, the leading foundations will have to modify their programs which now are mainly supportive. They will have to become more intimately and more enduringly involved in the creation and administration of projects. They will have to initiate, design, and staff projects and then supervise them, even though other institutions may carry them out. And they will have to be careful to overcome the traditional suspicion that they are attempting to usurp the role of other institutions, such as the university, and trying to use them for their own ends.

To make such changes, foundations must expand and upgrade their staff. They will have to overcome their traditional antipathy or indifference towards staffing discussed elsewhere in this book. Some foundations will have to enter the market for staff for the first time. Others will have to enter it for new people. All of them will have to seek out something better than those with manipulative administrative skills that characterize so many existing program officers. For the required staff, they will have to attract many more scholars with professional disciplines, both on a full-time basis and as consultants. Foundations may even find it helpful to bring in young people as trainees or interns, moving them, after a term of years, into other callings or professions. As I have pointed out earlier, highly qualified personnel are attracted to the more direct type of foundation program, and so the adoption of that type of program can be a factor in a successful talent search.

My advocating relatively radical program changes does not mean that the more conventional supportive programs should be ignored. Indeed there are areas where supportive foundation philanthropy should be more generous in the immediate future than it has been in the past. Many observers insist that the humanities and the arts, for example, as well as scientific, medical, and related research deserve more attention from foundations in the way of supportive grants. Especially is this held to be true of the immediate future because of the relative decline of government funding for training scientific manpower, equipment, and for ongoing research, brought on by the Vietnam War and the government's economic policy. Indeed how considerable the need for such conventional funding continues to be becomes apparent every time a university president appoints a vice president for development or the task force of some major commission on the future support of education makes its report.

To sum up, let us return to the question with which this chapter began, namely, whether the foundation can survive. To that question the answer at this point appears to be a qualified affirmative. Clearly whatever invasion there may be by the government of areas of activity traditionally reserved for the foundation, there appears to be no reason to fear that such invasion will so narrow philanthropic opportunity for the foundation as to make the foundation expendable. As we have noted on the preceding pages, the problems that invite foundation attention and action are as extensive and as demanding as at any time in the past. To the consideration and possible solution of these problems, foundations can contribute both limited financial resources and special institutional values neither of which either government or the public is likely to reject. Moreover foundations with even the most conventional program will continue to be favored as long as American society looks with favor upon a mixed system of private and public support for its cultural institutions.

Hence whatever doubts may persist as to the foundation's capacity for survival arise, then, from other considerations. The more important of these may be summarized as follows: (1) the danger of continued abuse of the foundation instrument by a relative minority which could bring on even more severe regulation than that recently experienced and adversely affect all foundations; (2) laxity on the part of the foundation community in discharging the responsibility of putting its own house in order and effectively policing itself; and (3) above all, inability or unwillingness to mount the kind of program or to develop the staff and managerial know-how that are needed to cope successfully with the philanthropic challenges that now confront foundations. If, therefore, we end on a note of optimism, it must be a note of guarded optimism.

INDEX